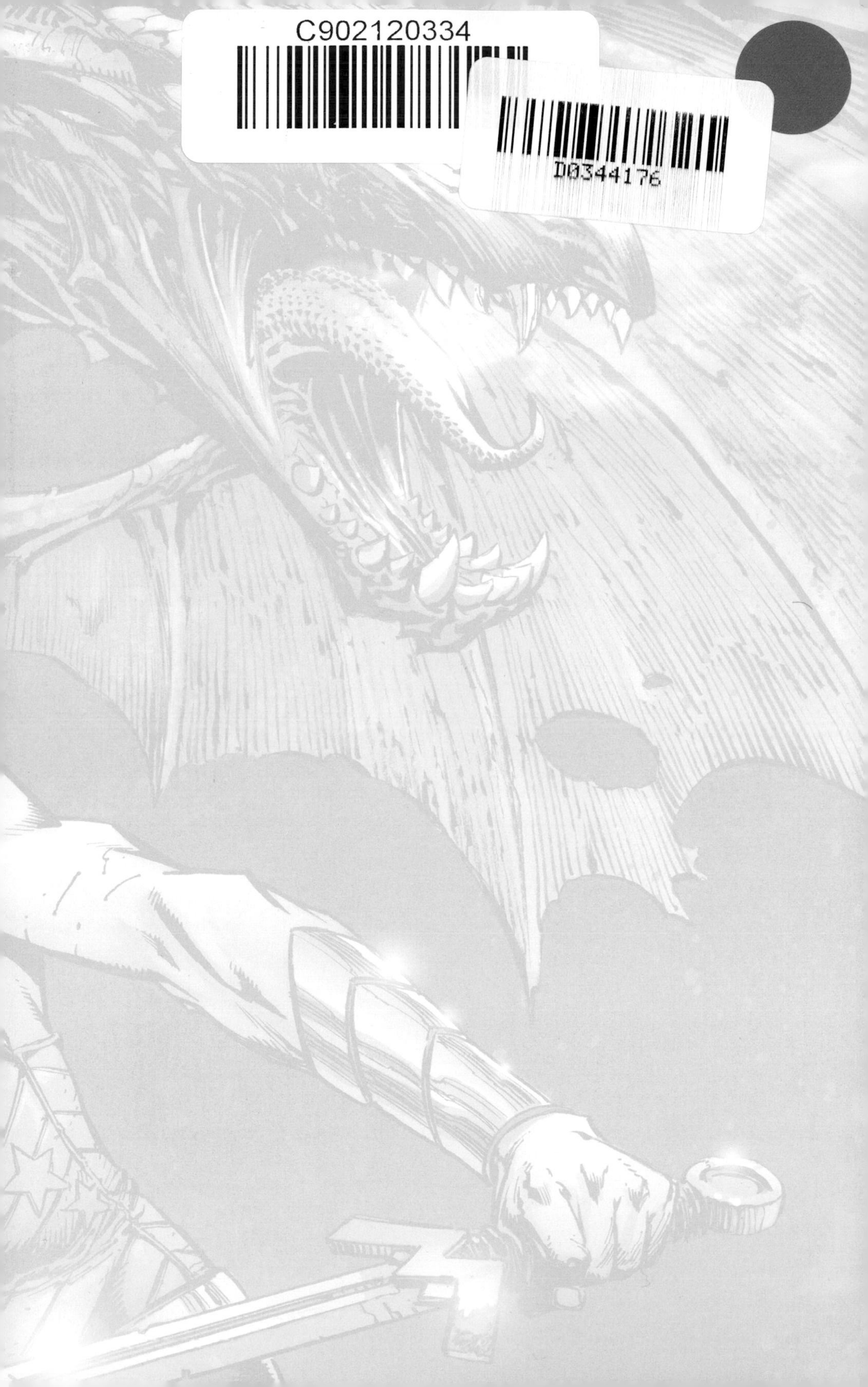

WONDER WOMAN™

WARRIOR FOR JUSTICE

Written by Liz Marsham

Wonder Woman created by William Moulton Marston

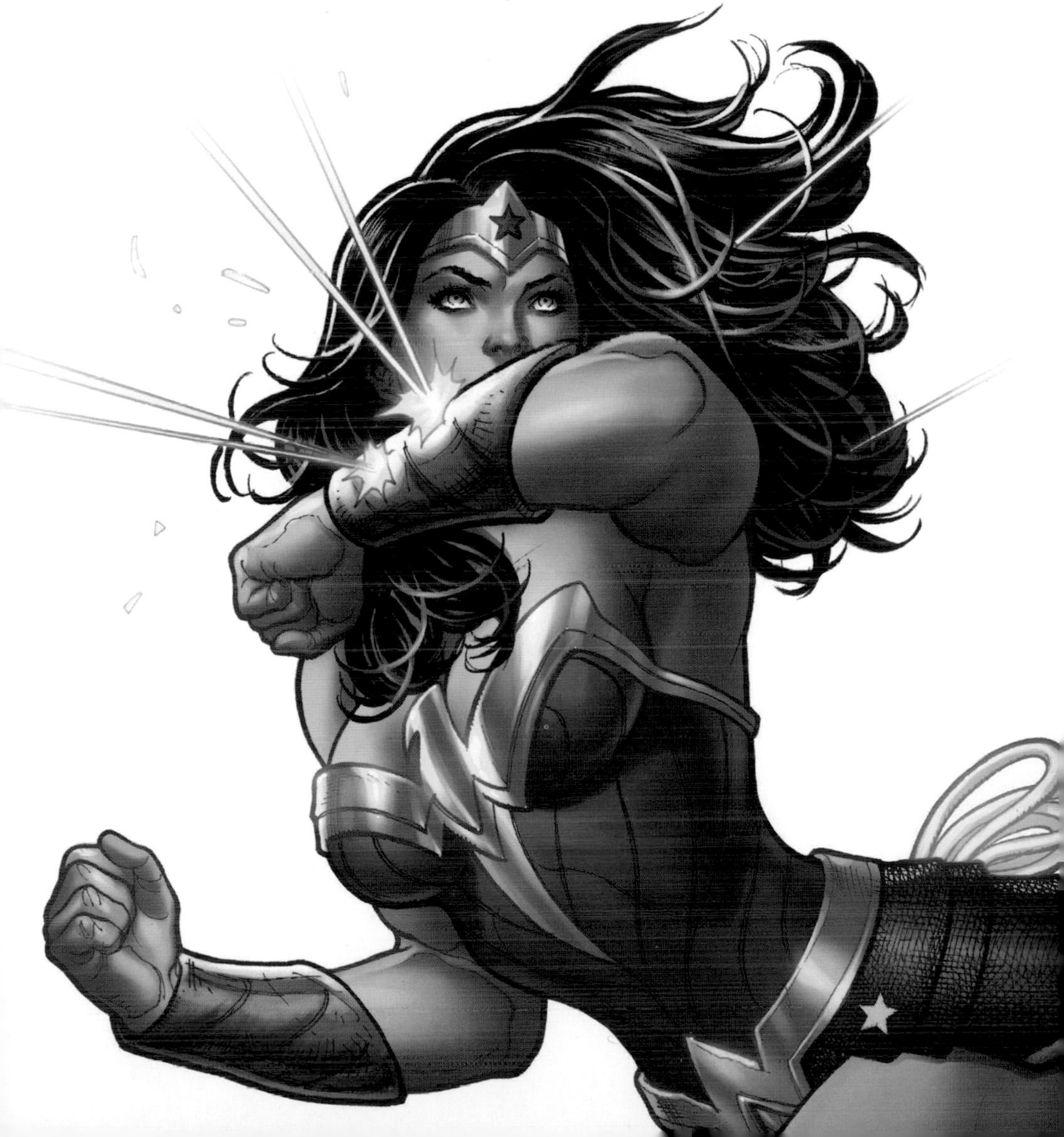

Editor Lauren Nesworthy
Designer Lisa Rogers
Pre-production Producer Siu Chan
Producer Zara Markland
Managing Editor Sadie Smith
Managing Art Editor Ron Stobbart
Publisher Julie Ferris
Art Director Lisa Lanzarini
Publishing Director Simon Beecroft

Reading Consultant Maureen Fernandes

First published in Great Britain in 2017
by Dorling Kindersley Limited
80 Strand, London WC2R 0RL
A Penguin Random House Company

10 9 8 7 6 5 4 3 2 1
001–299068–May/2017

A CIP catalogue record for this book
is available from the British Library.

ISBN: 978-0-24128-519-0

Printed in China

A WORLD OF IDEAS:
SEE ALL THERE IS TO KNOW

www.dk.com
www.dccomics.com

Contents

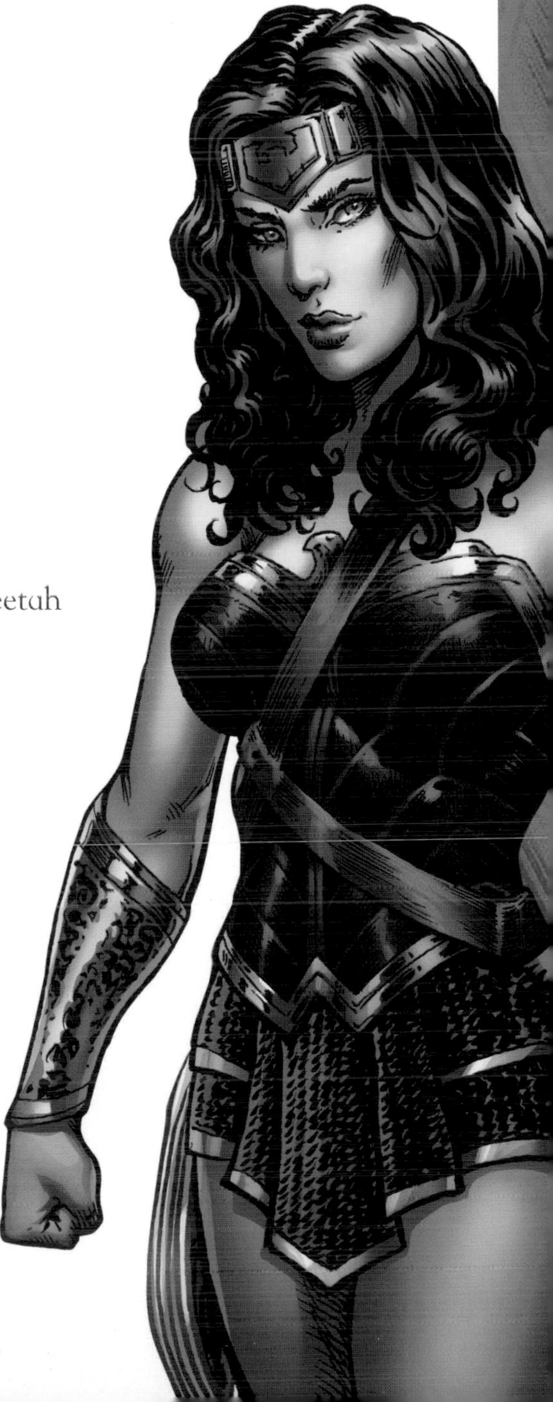

A TRUE HERO

She is Princess Diana of the Amazons. She is as strong as Superman and as wise as Batman. She can run like the wind and fly like a bird. She is an enemy to those who would make war, and a hero for the whole world.

She is Wonder Woman!

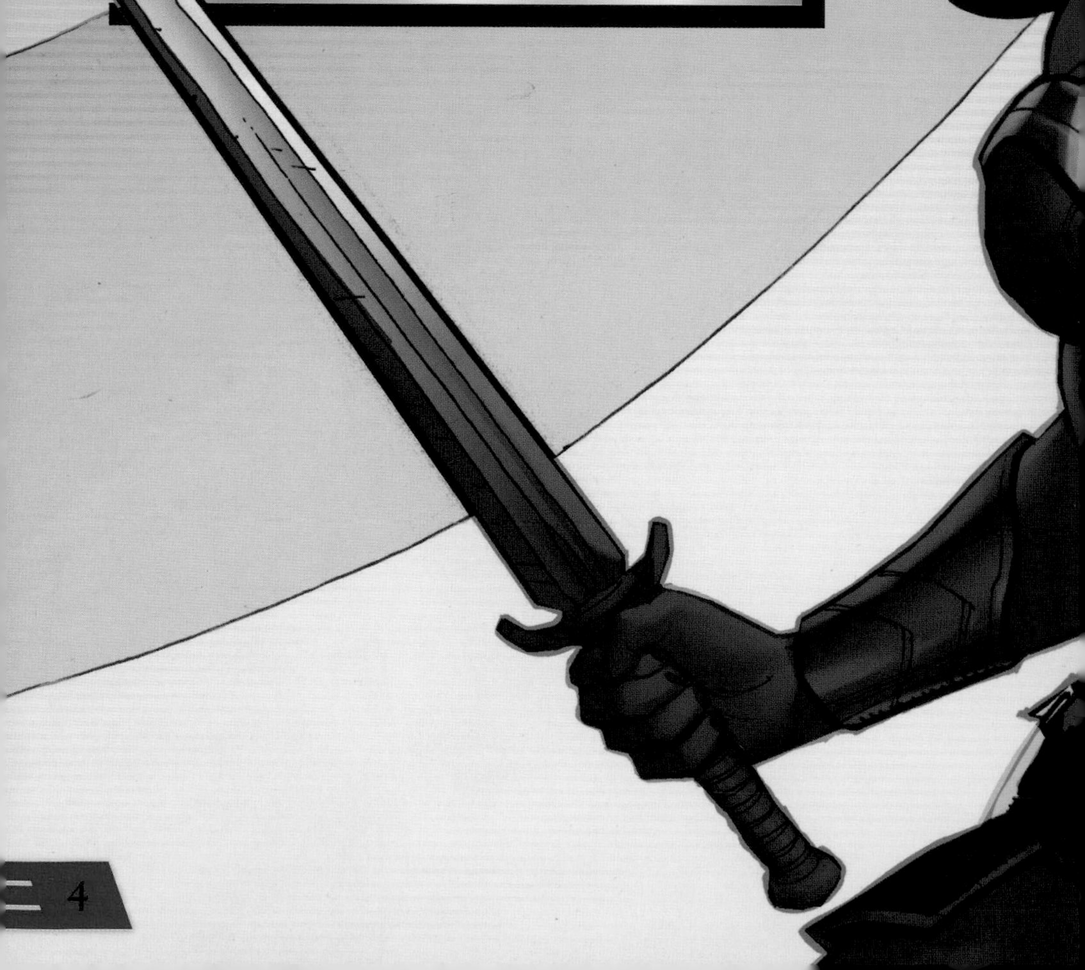

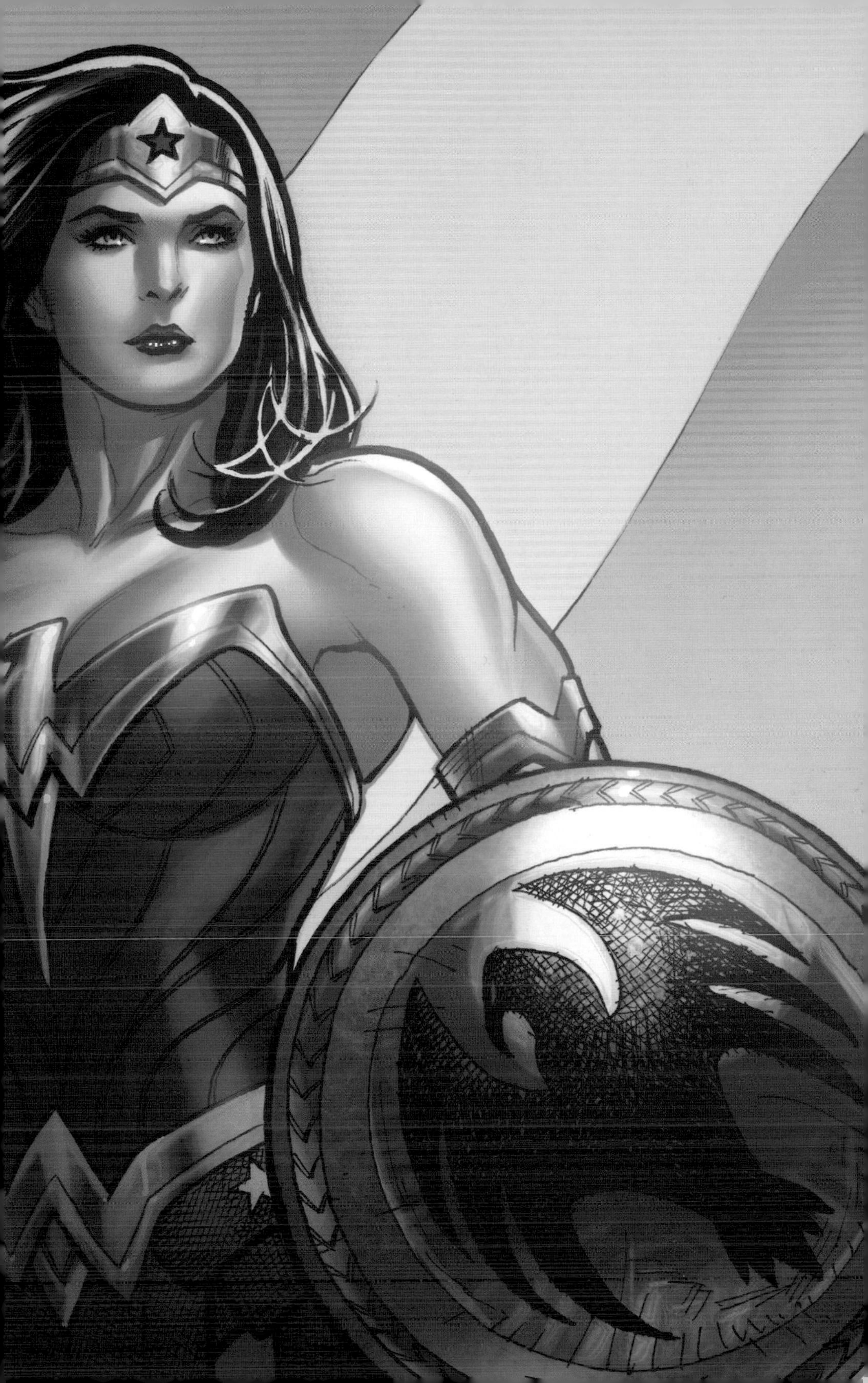

Wonder Woman's Mission

Wonder Woman is one of the most powerful Super Heroes on Earth!

She believes in peace and equality, so she would rather talk than fight. She knows that dealing with people fairly is the best way to solve problems. However, she is always prepared to use her incredible strength and skills as a warrior to protect those in need. Sometimes the battles are hard, but Wonder Woman never gives in to fear. It takes great courage to face such powerful enemies!

Wonder Woman doesn't just tell everyone what she stands for; she shows them. This makes her a strong leader – and an even stronger hero.

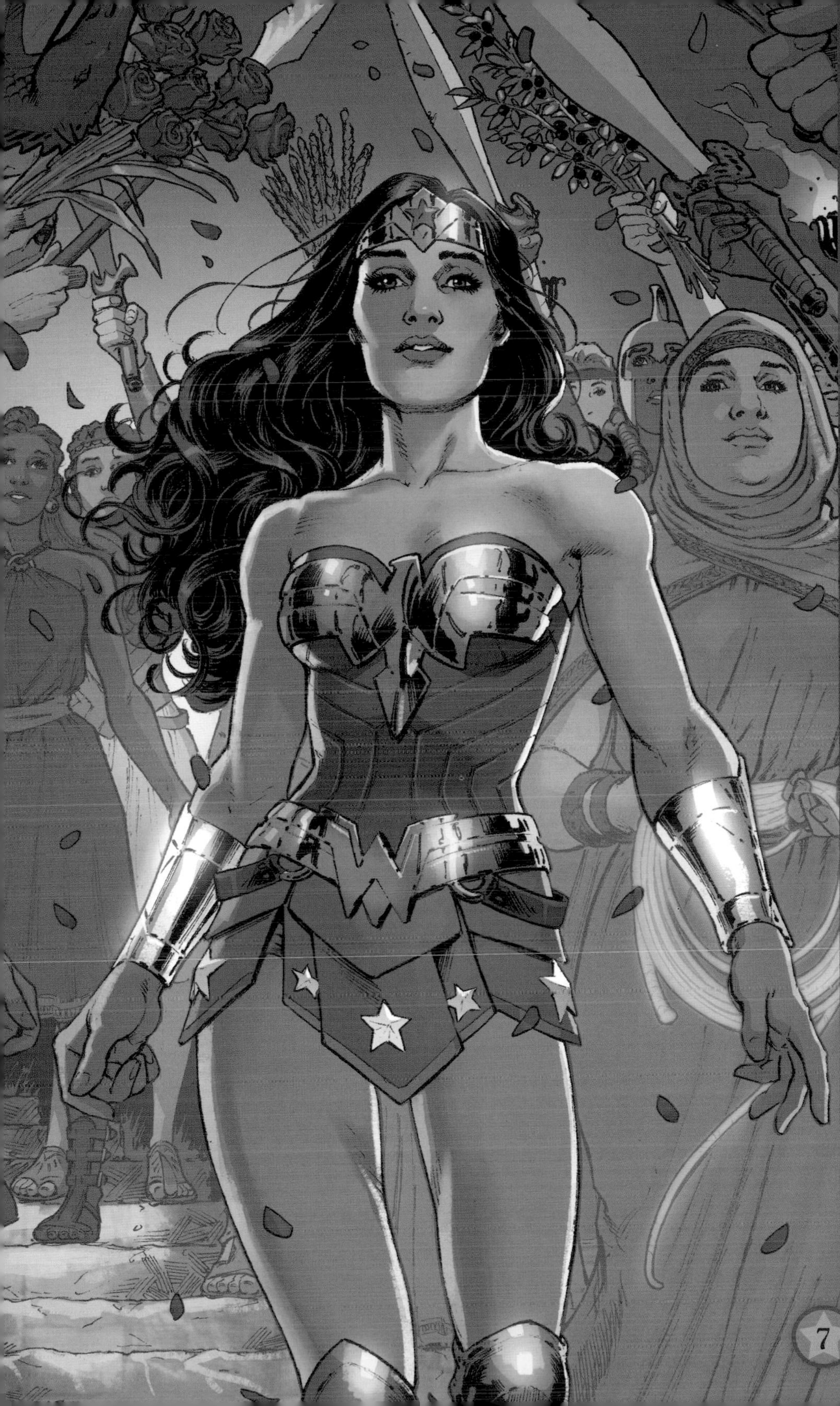

Living in Paradise

Many years ago, the Greek gods decided to bless one island and keep it separate from the rest of the world. They created Themyscira (Them-mes-skera), also known as Paradise Island.

A tribe of women, called the Amazons, lives on the beautiful island, far away from any other country. As the centuries pass, the Amazons never age or die. They live without electricity and other modern technology. While they are trained as warriors, they live in peace.

Before Wonder Woman devoted her life to protecting Earth, Themyscira was her home.

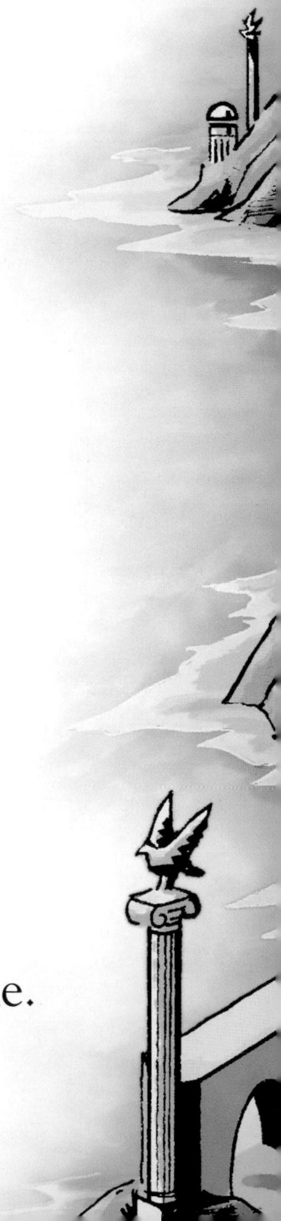

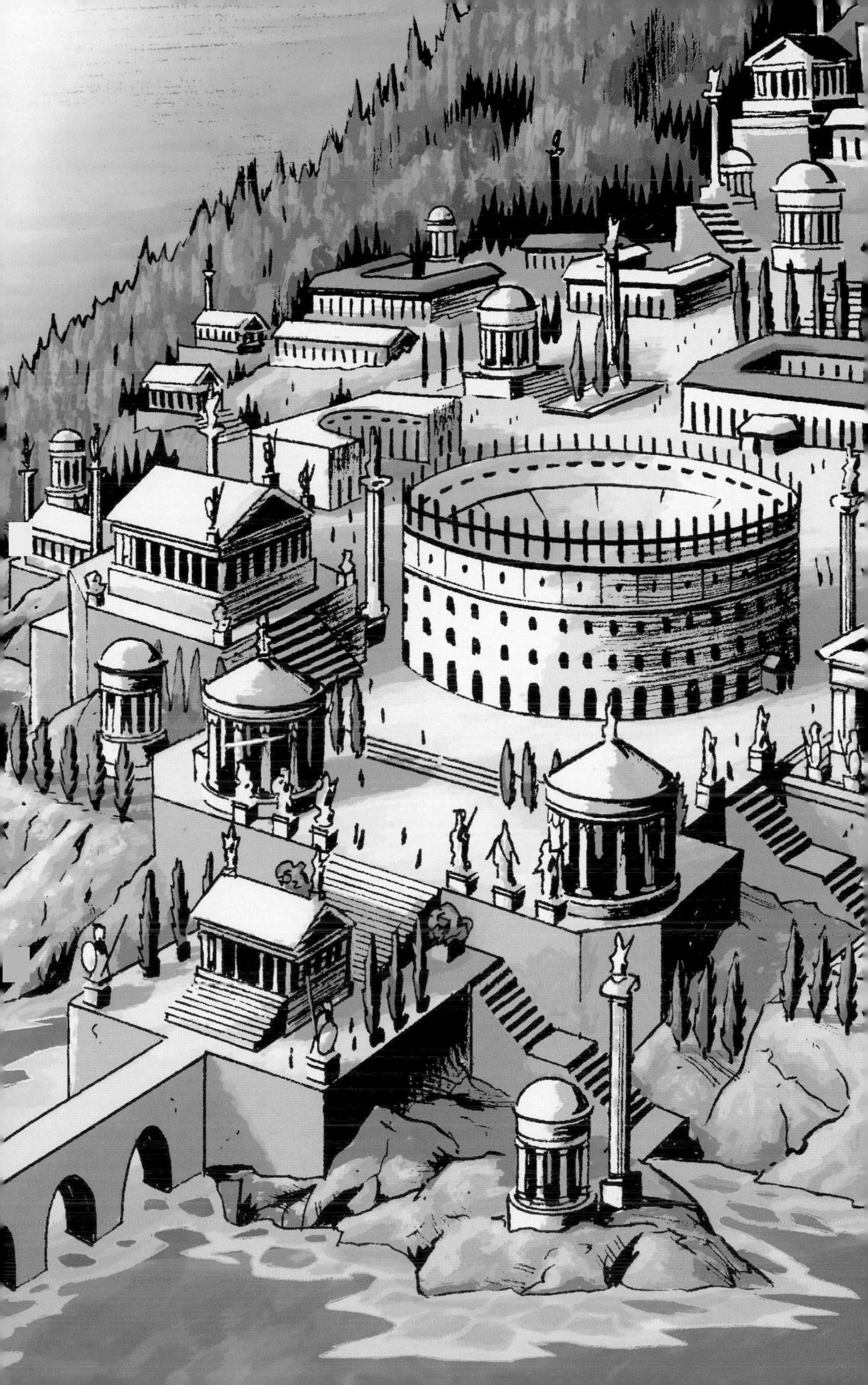

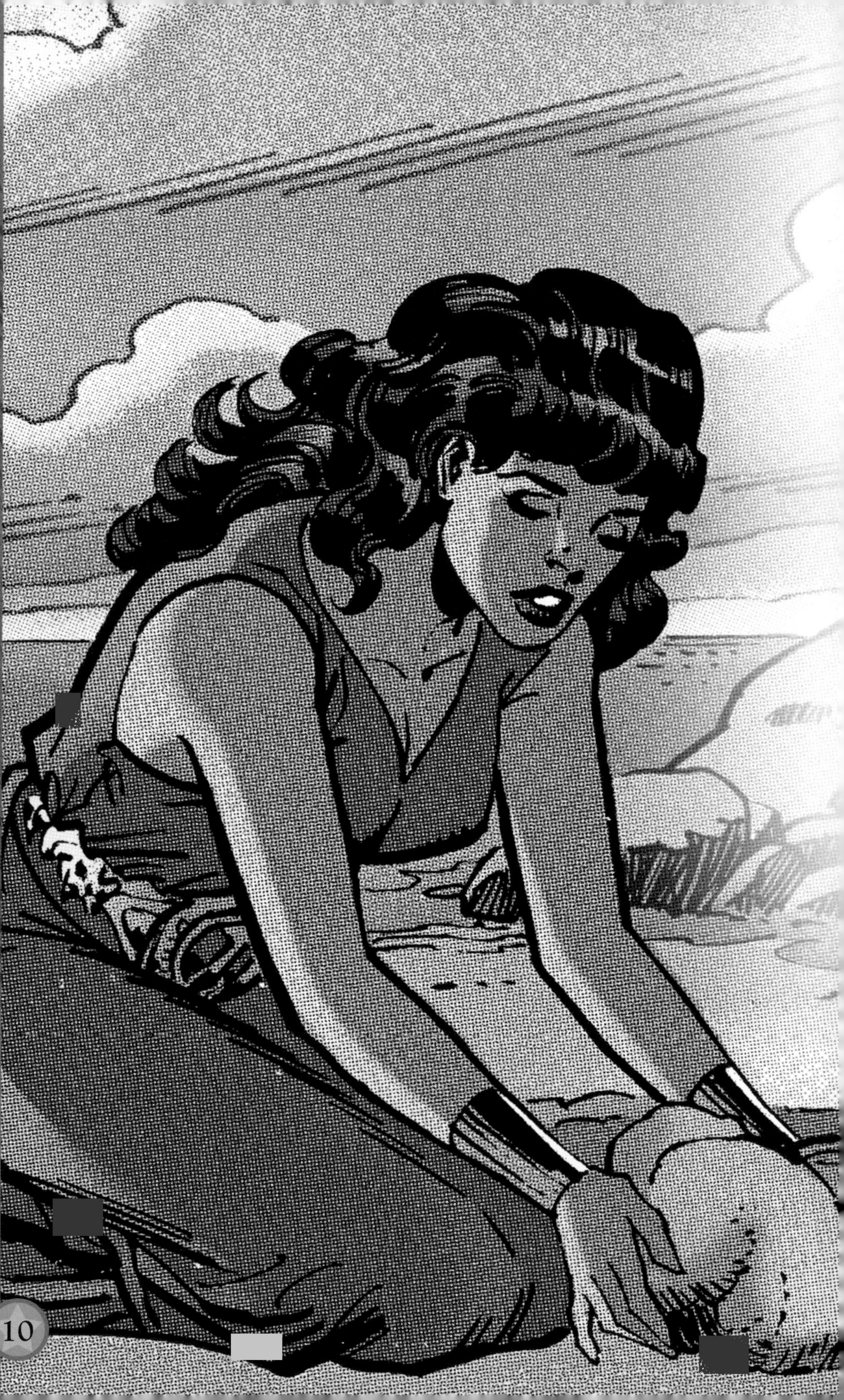

A Royal Birth

The Amazons are ruled by the wise and fair Queen Hippolyta (Hi-poli-ta). The queen wanted a child, and prayed to the gods to help her. One night, the gods granted Hippolyta's wish. They told her that she must form a

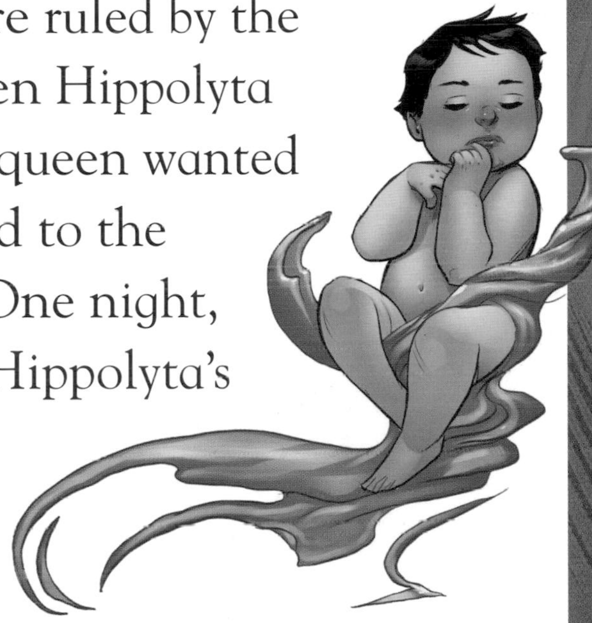

child out of the island itself. Hippolyta knelt on the seashore and scooped up handful after handful of wet clay. Soon she had sculpted a baby girl.

The gods reached down and touched the clay, and the baby came to life! Hippolyta was overjoyed, and she named her new daughter Diana.

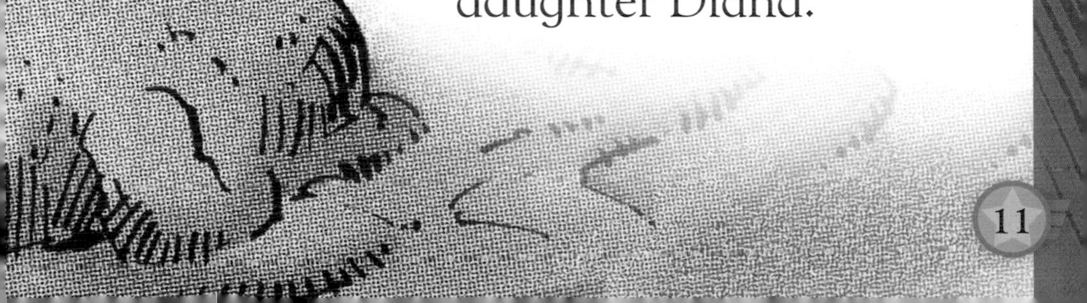

Growing Up

The young Princess Diana was loved by all the Amazons. They taught her to ride and hunt, to be imaginative and curious. They taught her to fight well, but to avoid fighting when she could.

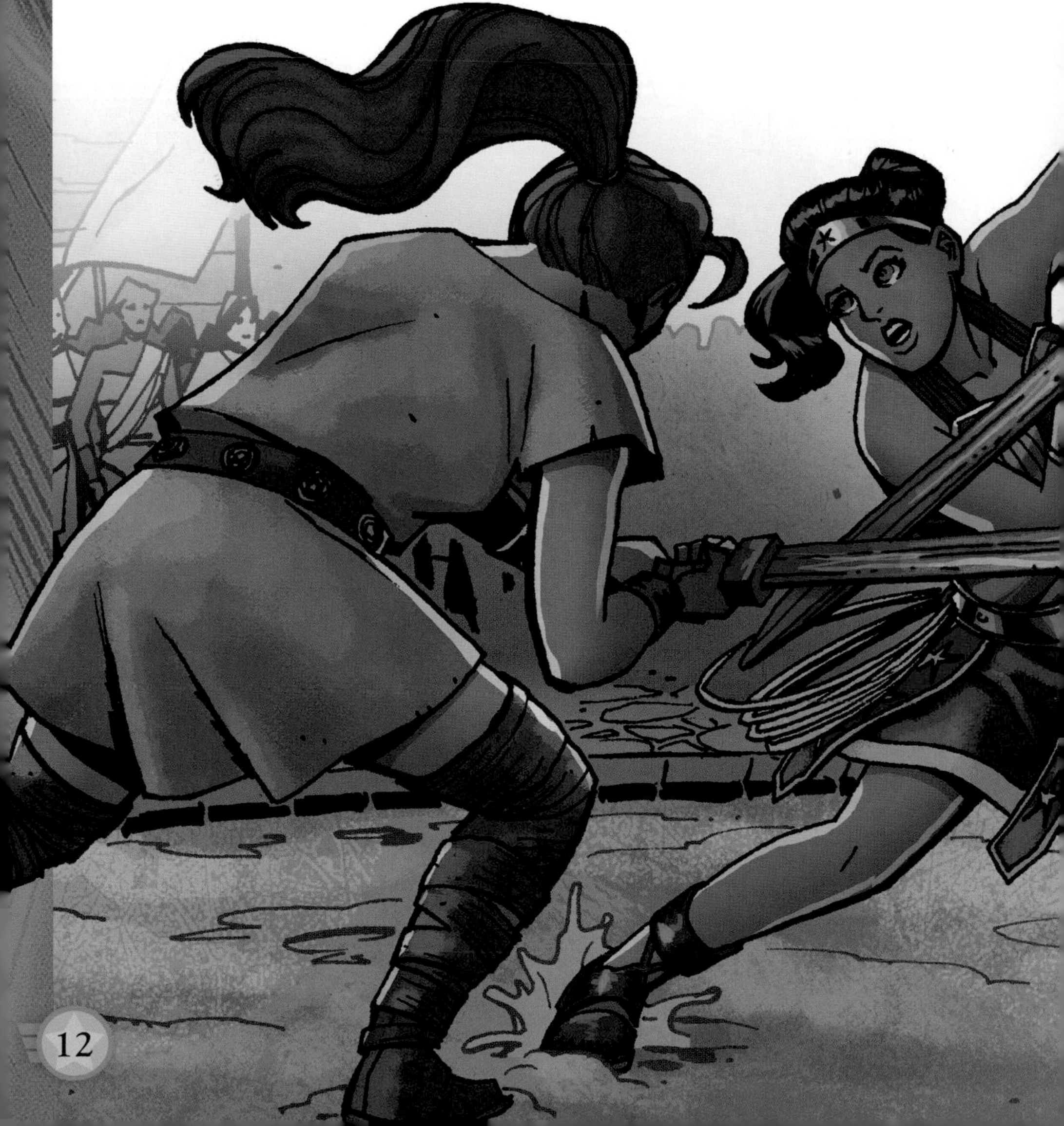

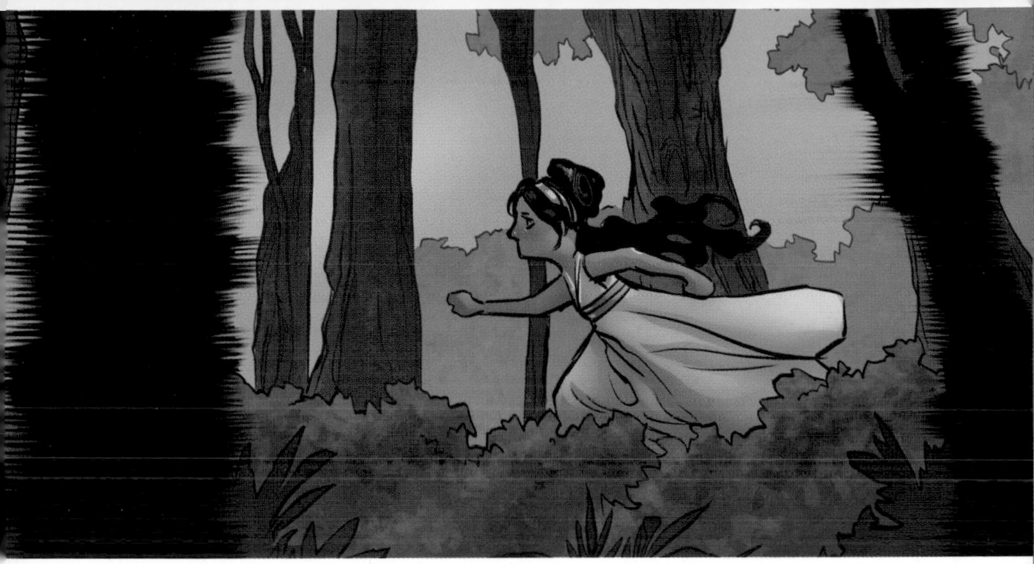

They taught her to solve problems creatively and love all living things. Diana learned quickly, and soon she was debating with the best thinkers and training with the best warriors on the island. She explored Themyscira until she knew every inch by heart. She loved everything about her home. But Diana could not stop wondering... what else was out there?

Becoming a Hero

As the years passed, the Amazons realised that they could not hide from the world forever. Planes flew in the sky, and satellites were mapping the Earth. It was only a matter of time before humans would find Paradise Island.

Hippolyta declared a tournament to find the strongest, fastest and smartest of

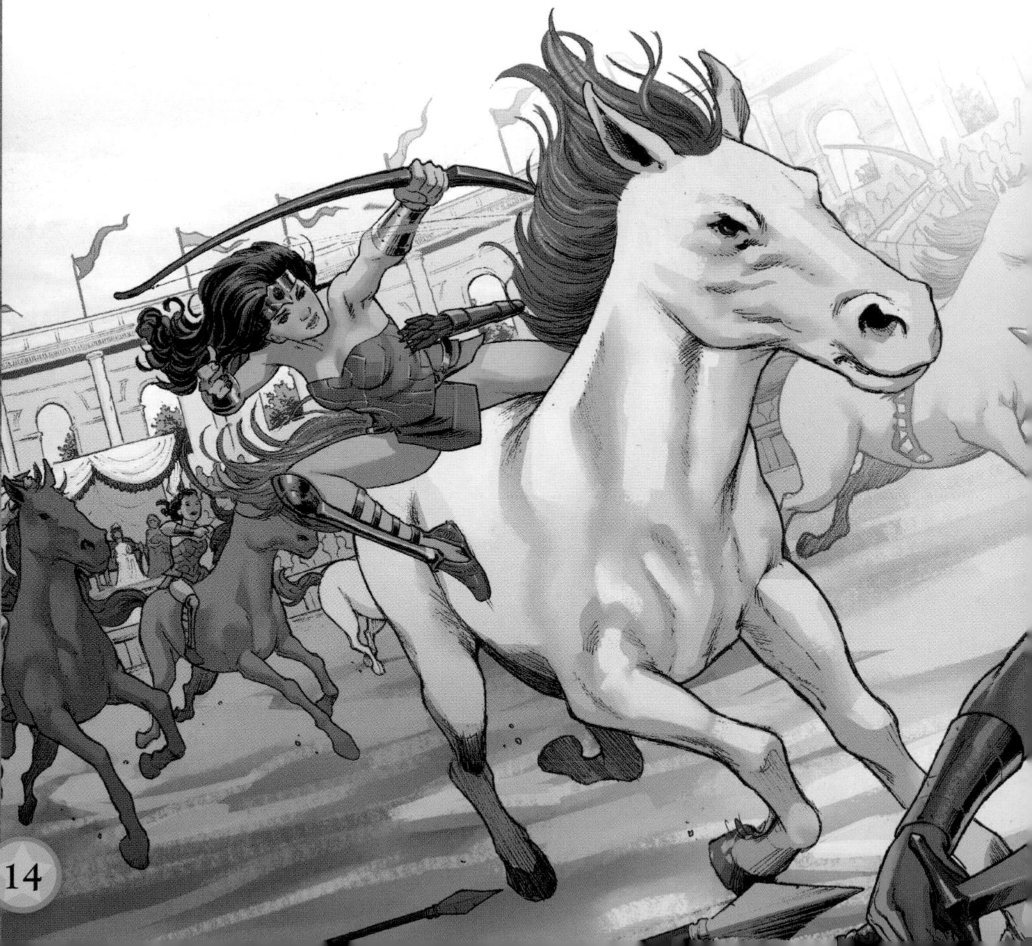

the Amazons. The winner would be sent out as an ambassador, to represent Paradise Island in the rest of the world.

Diana won every event in the tournament. It was time for her to meet the world – and for the world to meet Wonder Woman!

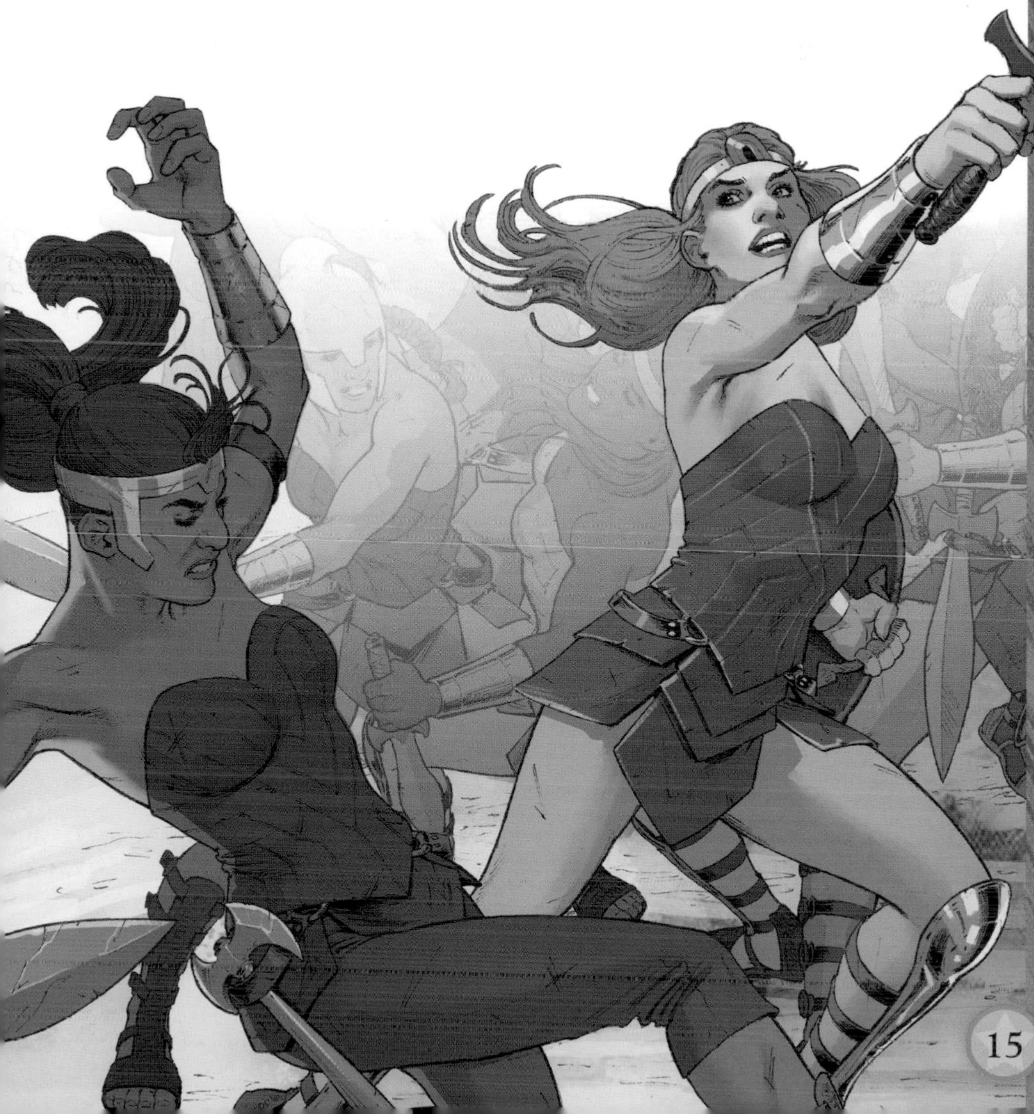

THE GODS

★ OF THE AMAZONS ★

The Amazons worship many powerful Greek gods. Each god or goddess has special abilities, which they can pass on to those who deserve them. Some gods have helped Wonder Woman by granting her the powers that she needs in her fight for justice.

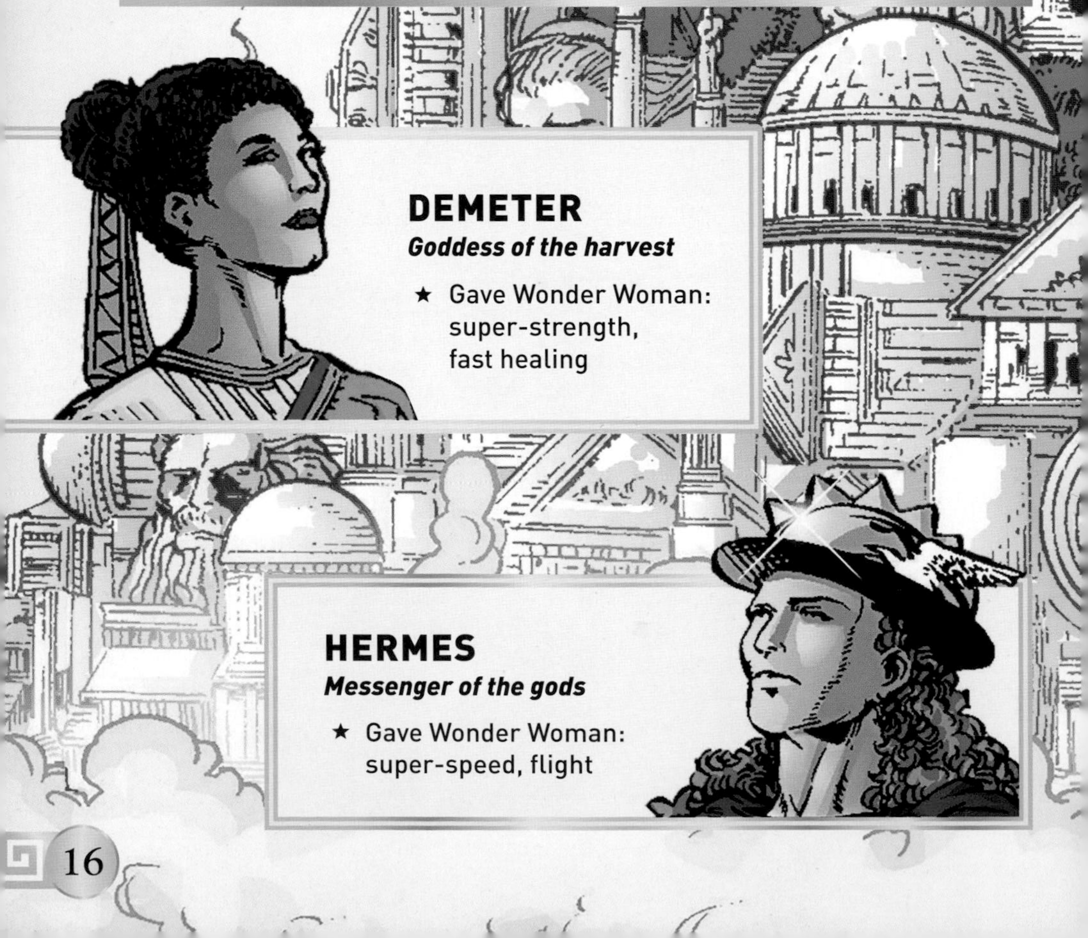

DEMETER

Goddess of the harvest

★ Gave Wonder Woman: super-strength, fast healing

HERMES

Messenger of the gods

★ Gave Wonder Woman: super-speed, flight

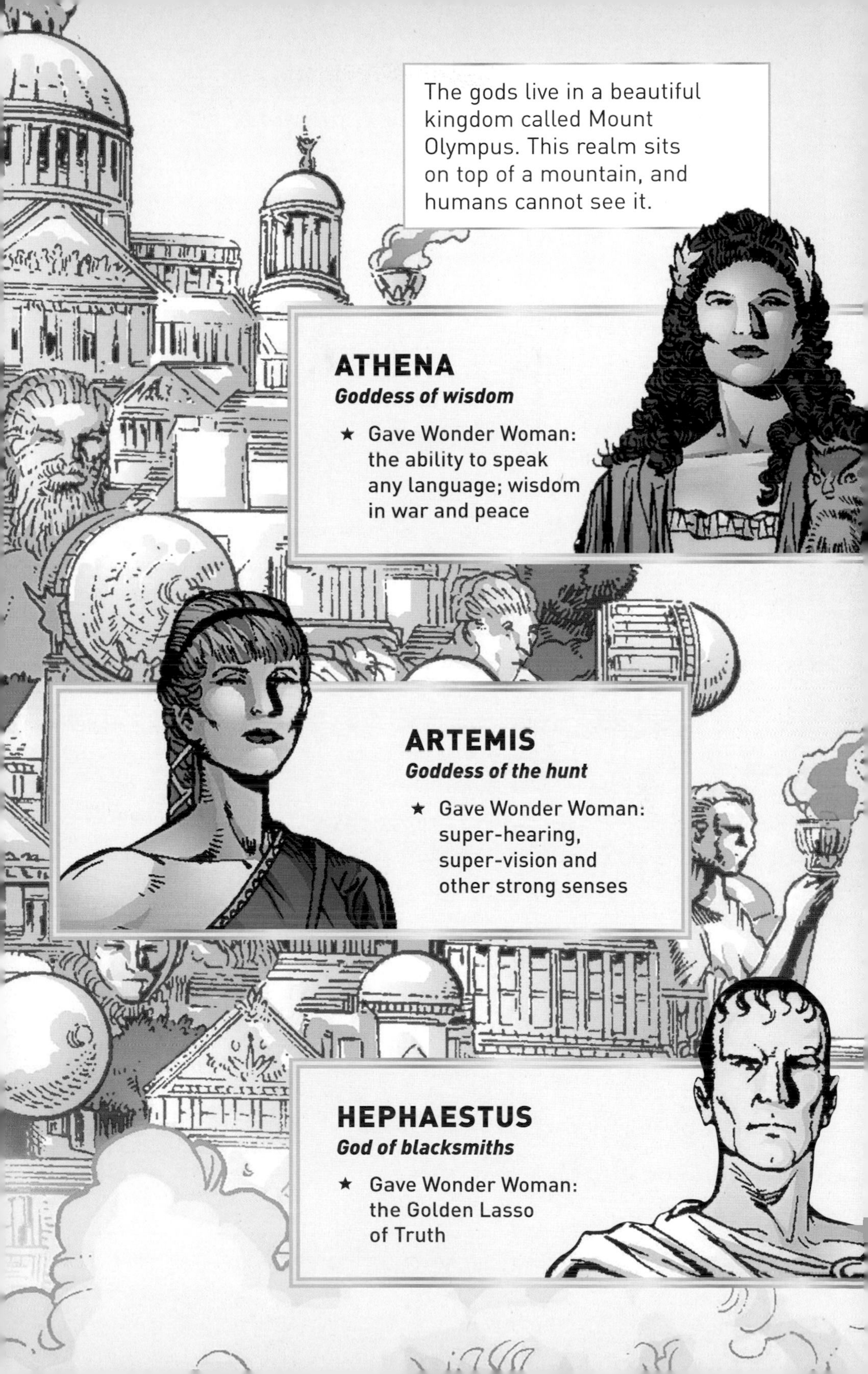

The gods live in a beautiful kingdom called Mount Olympus. This realm sits on top of a mountain, and humans cannot see it.

ATHENA

Goddess of wisdom

★ Gave Wonder Woman: the ability to speak any language; wisdom in war and peace

ARTEMIS

Goddess of the hunt

★ Gave Wonder Woman: super-hearing, super-vision and other strong senses

HEPHAESTUS

God of blacksmiths

★ Gave Wonder Woman: the Golden Lasso of Truth

Bracelets from a Goddess

Most of the Amazons wear large silver bracelets on both wrists. However, Wonder Woman's bracelets are particularly unique!

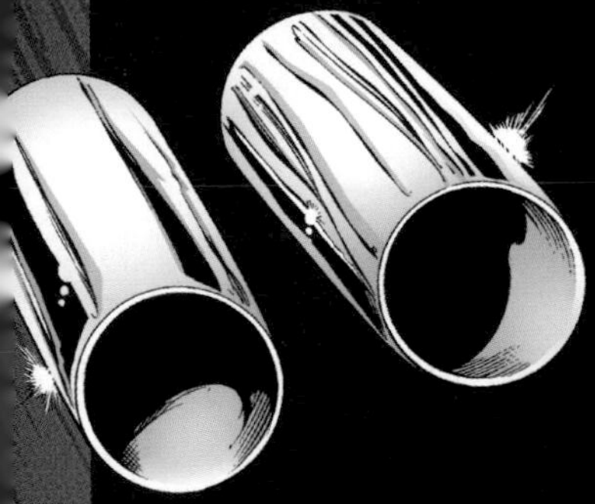

When Diana won the tournament on Paradise Island, she was given a special reward: bracelets made from the shield of Athena, the goddess of wisdom. These magical bands cannot be destroyed. Bullets, energy blasts and lasers bounce right off of them.

When Wonder Woman slams the bracelets together, they create a powerful wave of energy that knocks her enemies off their feet.

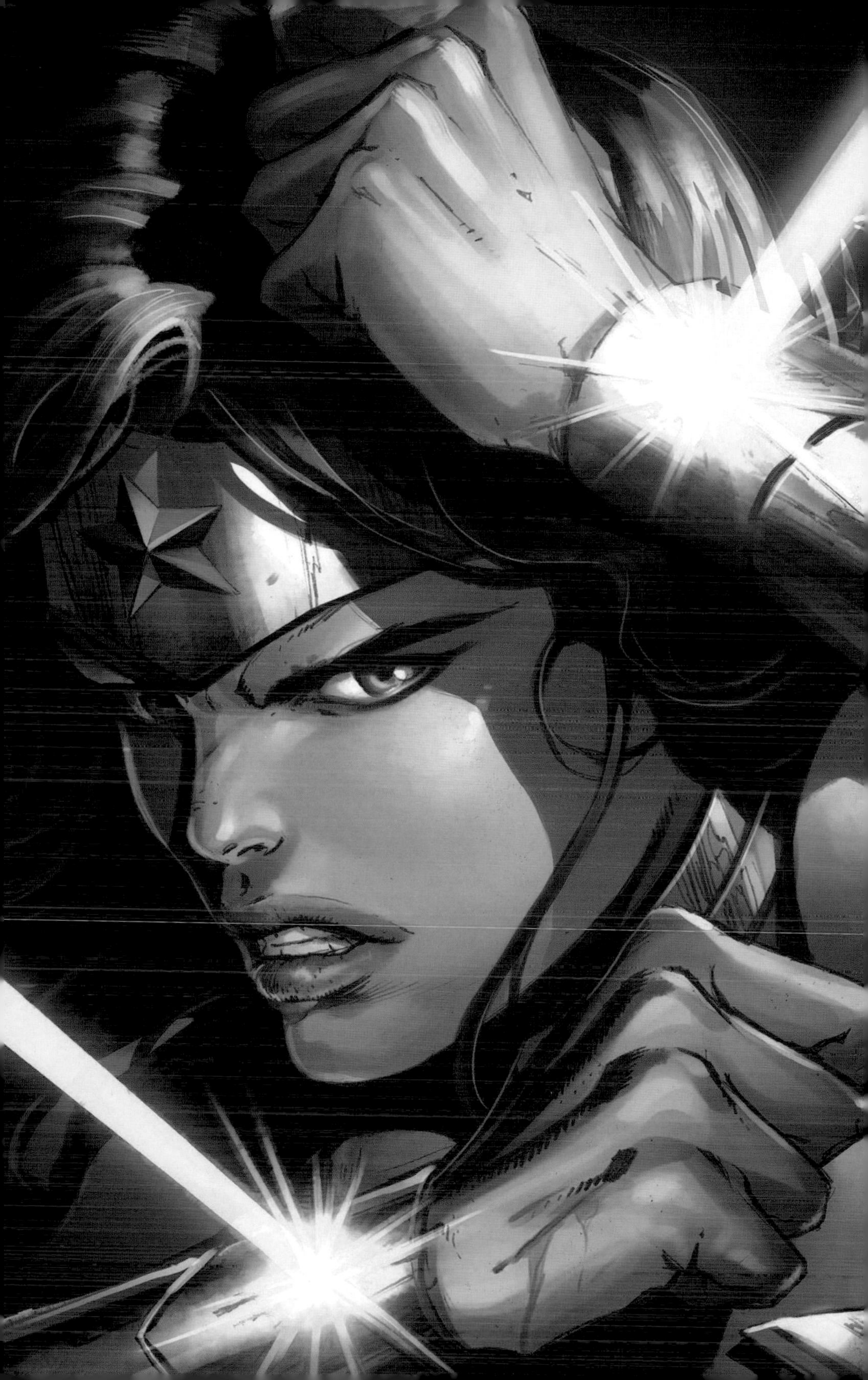

The Golden Lasso of Truth

Wonder Woman's most important weapon is her Golden Lasso of Truth. She uses it to grab and tie up enemies – but she could use any piece of rope for that. The lasso is much more special.

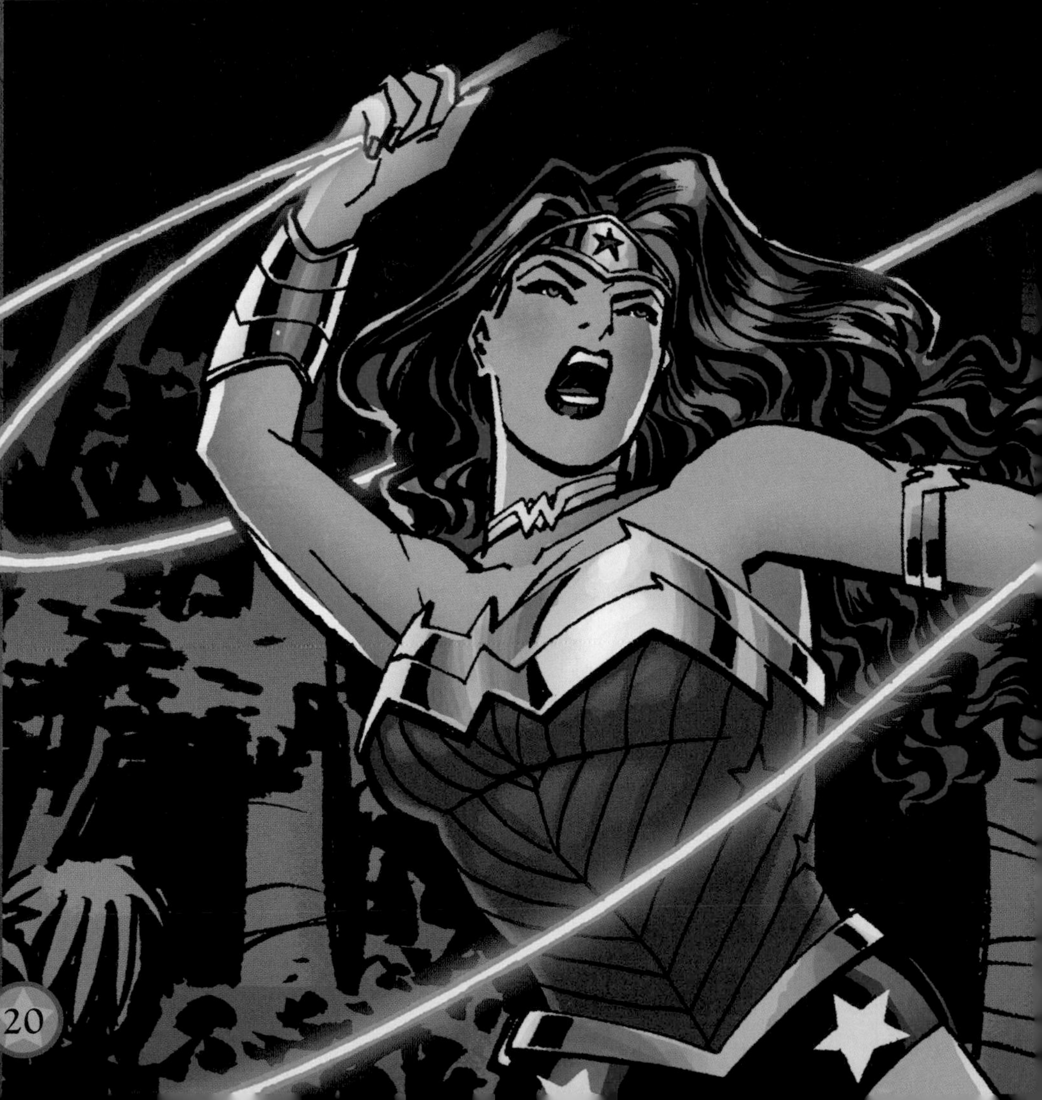

This magical rope can be as long or as short as Wonder Woman wants it to be. It is so strong that not even Superman can break it. Strangest and most wonderful of all, anyone caught in the lasso must tell the complete truth. With this powerful weapon in her hand, villains can't hide any secrets from Wonder Woman!

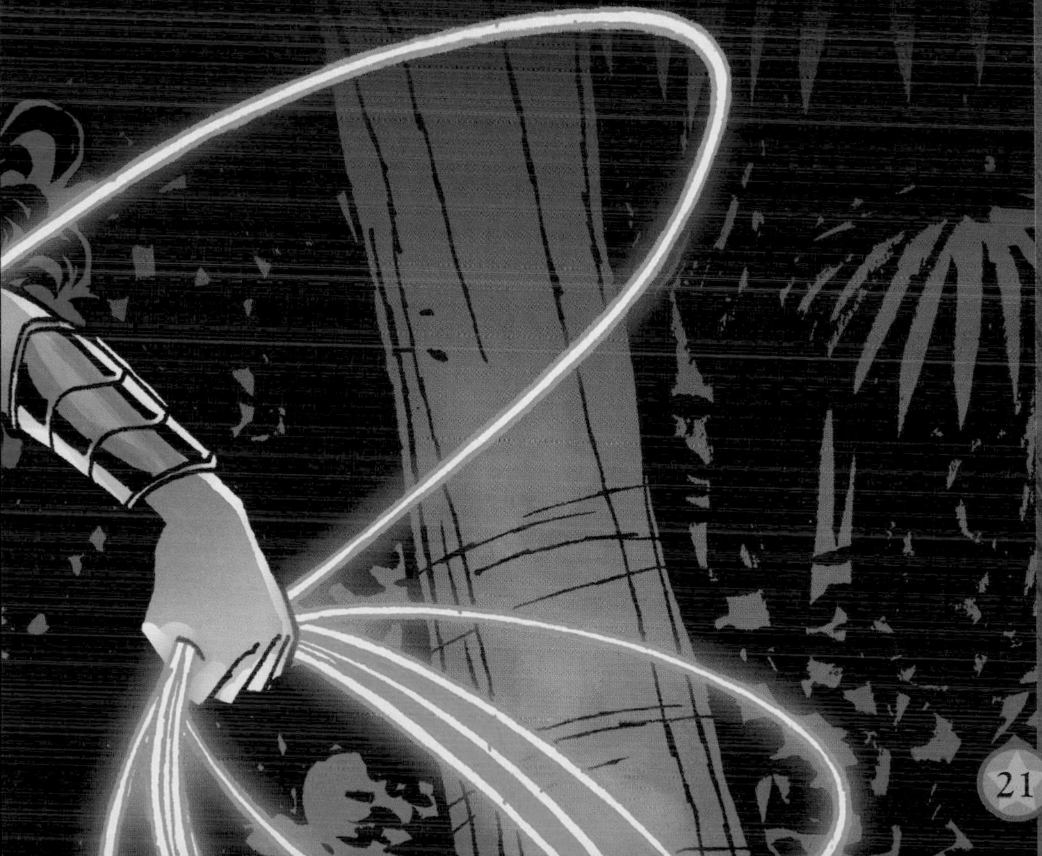

ELEMENTS OF A WARRIOR

As the world's most powerful warrior, Wonder Woman is equipped with the best armor, tools and weapons. She is always prepared for battle!

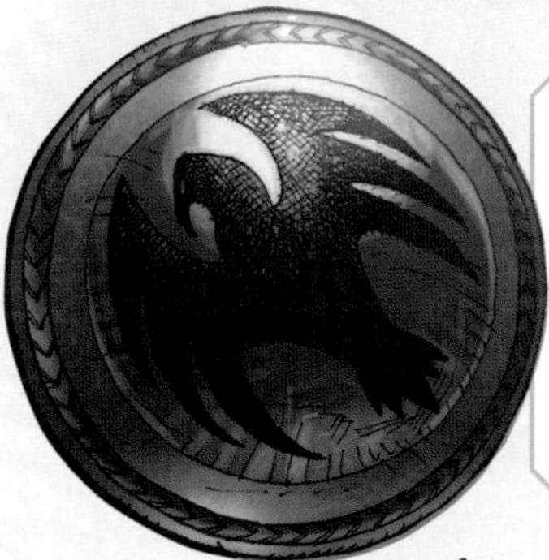

WEAPONS OF CHOICE

- Skilled with all weaponry
- Prefers traditional Amazonian weapons, such as swords and shields
- Avoids human weapons, such as guns
- Uses mostly close-range weapons so she can lead others into battle

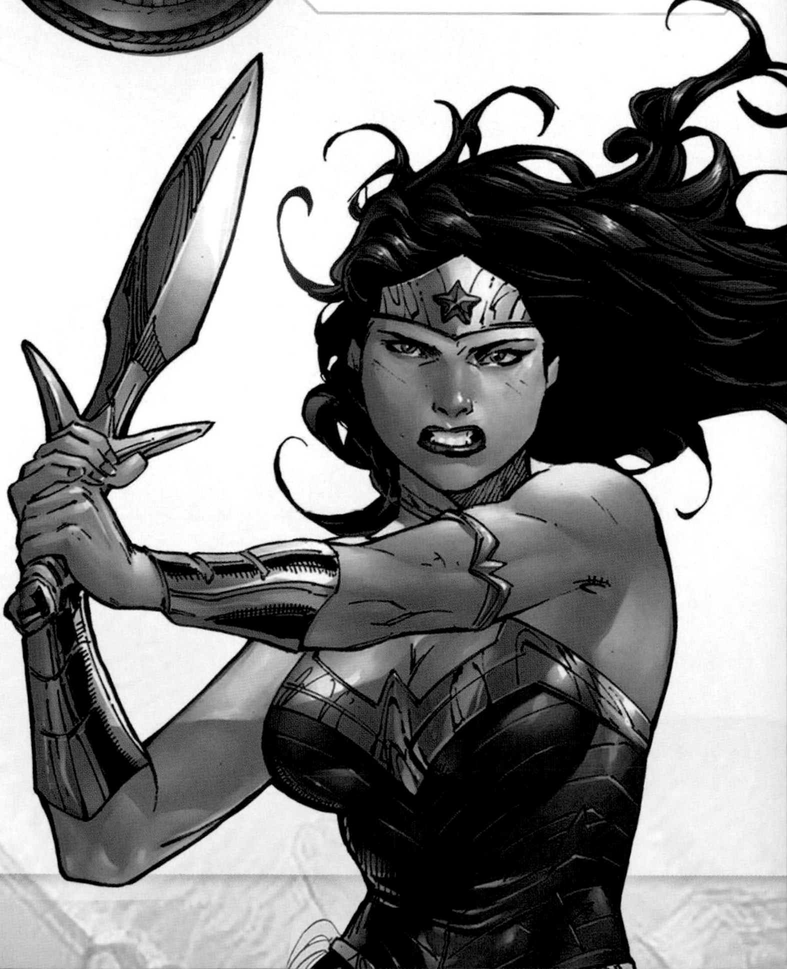

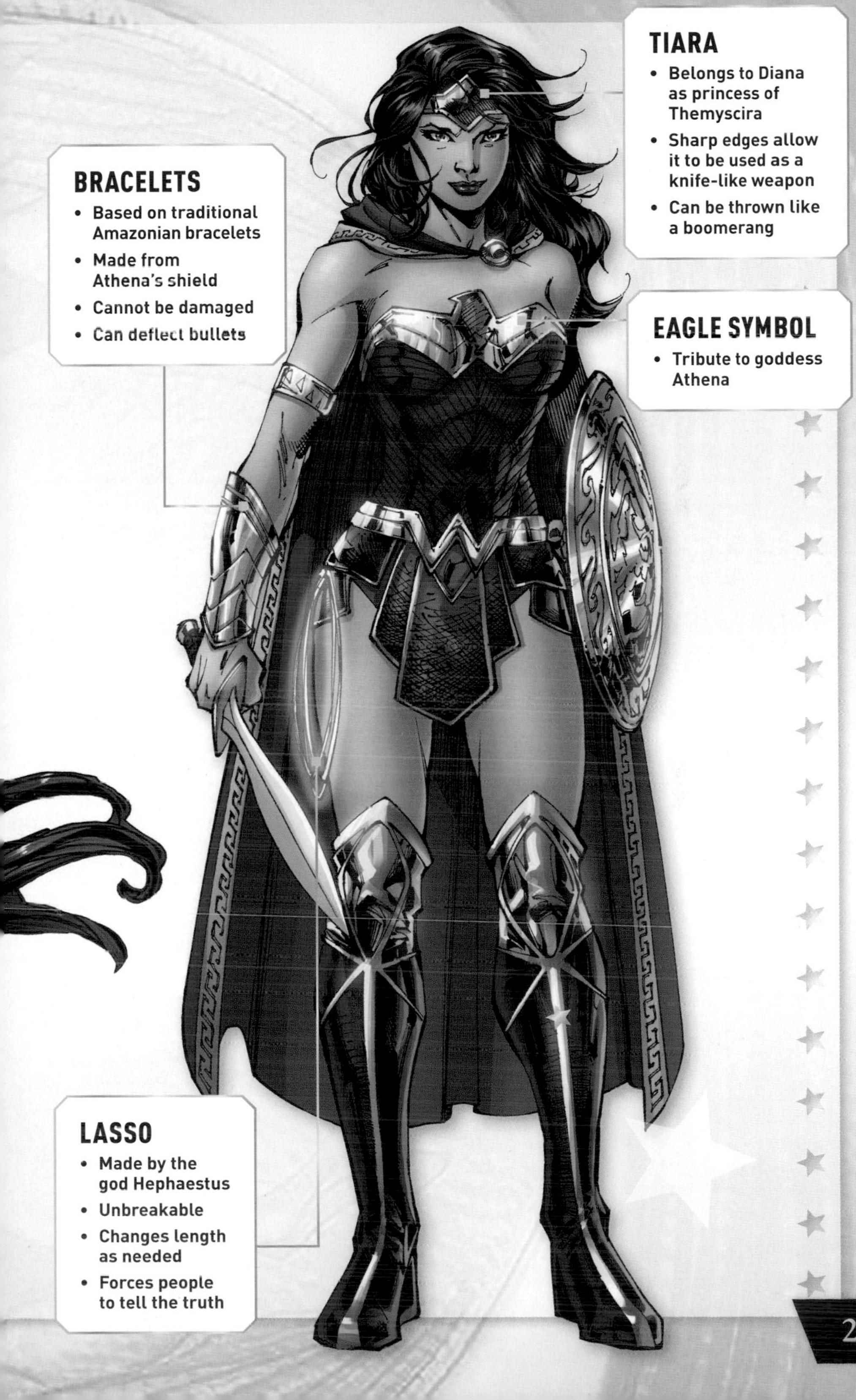
TIARA
• Belongs to Diana as princess of Themyscira
• Sharp edges allow it to be used as a knife-like weapon
• Can be thrown like a boomerang
BRACELETS
• Based on traditional Amazonian bracelets
• Made from Athena's shield
• Cannot be damaged
• Can deflect bullets
EAGLE SYMBOL
• Tribute to goddess Athena
LASSO
• Made by the god Hephaestus
• Unbreakable
• Changes length as needed
• Forces people to tell the truth

Strength and Speed

When Diana was born, the gods granted her many special powers.

Demeter, goddess of the harvest, gave Diana enormous strength. Wonder Woman can hold an aeroplane over her head and crush rocks with her bare hands.

Demeter also gave Wonder Woman the ability to heal quickly from any injury. She has even survived being thrown into the Sun!

Thanks to Hermes, the gods' messenger, Wonder Woman can move incredibly fast. She can even speed past a moving bullet.

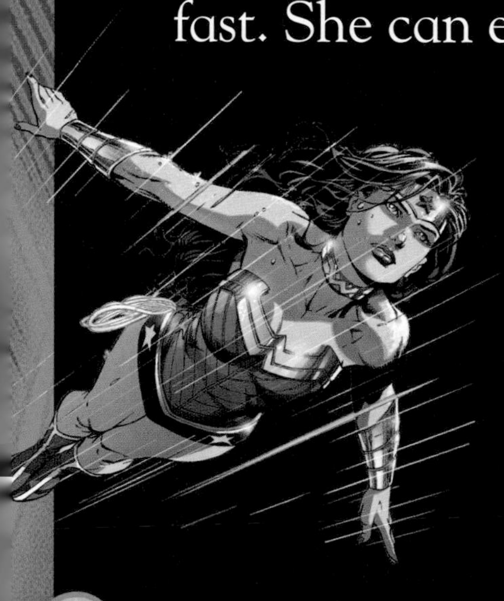

Hermes also granted Wonder Woman the ability to fly. She can zoom around the world to wherever she is needed most!

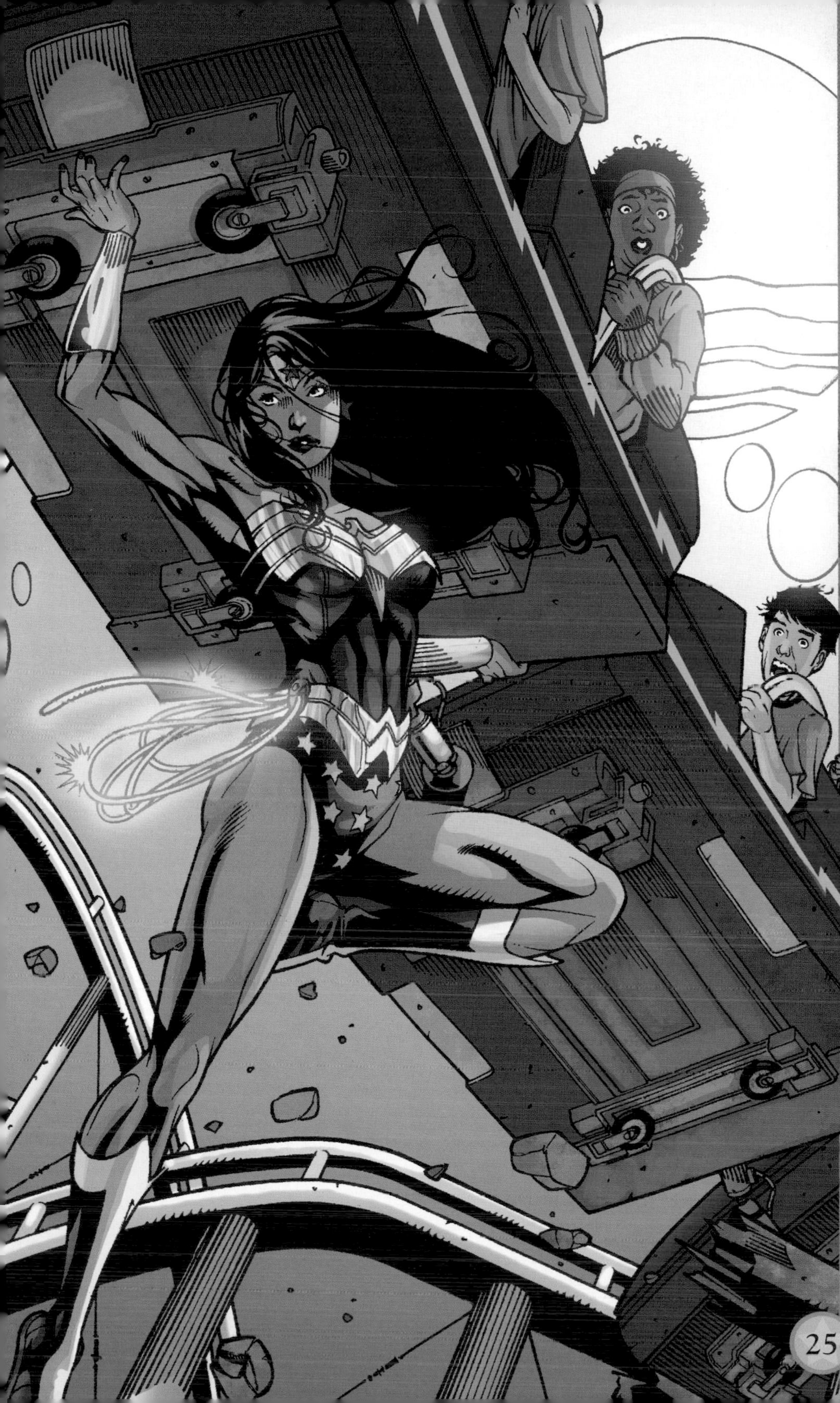

Super Senses and Wisdom

Artemis, the goddess of the hunt, made Wonder Woman's senses super-powerful. She can see great distances and she can hear the softest sound from far away. She can track her enemies from the vibrations of their feet and the movement of the air as they run.

Donna
Troy

Wonder
Woman

From Athena, the goddess of wisdom, Wonder Woman received the ability to speak all languages. This is very useful when combined with Athena's other gift: great wisdom in both war and peace. This means that Wonder Woman is excellent at planning and leading battles, arranging peace talks and making friends with anyone, on any planet.

Cassie
Sandsmark

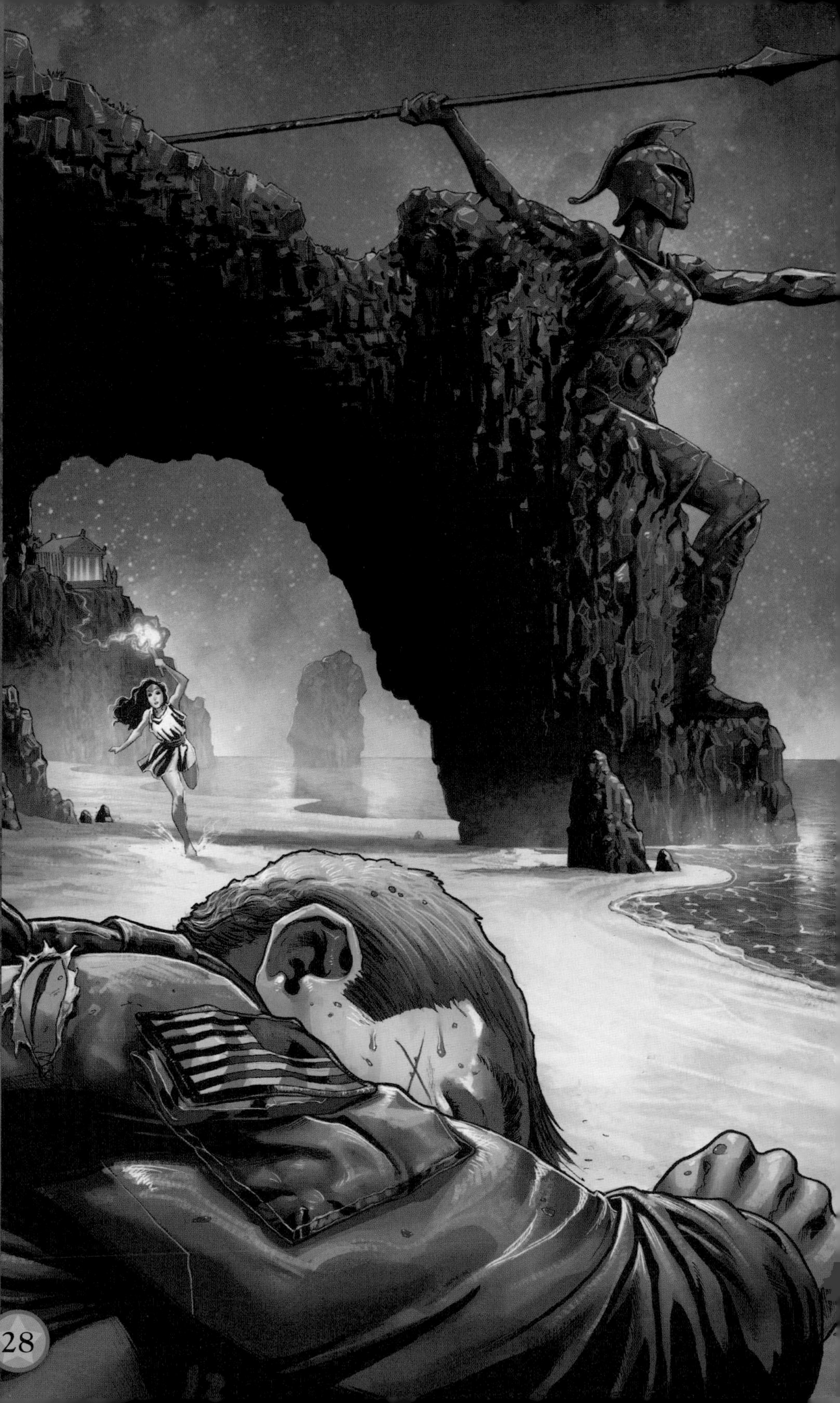

A Human Friend

Before the Amazons sent Diana out into the modern world, the modern world found them. An American military plane crashed onto Paradise Island! Diana rushed to help the pilot, who introduced himself as Steve Trevor.

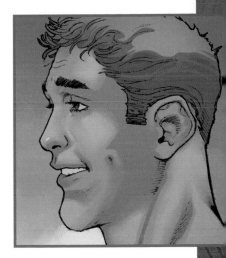

While Steve healed, the two became friends. When he was ready to leave the island, they made a deal. To repay her for rescuing him, Steve would introduce Wonder Woman to America.

Now, when the US government wants to talk to Wonder Woman, they go through Steve. Steve is always happy to fight crime with her. Sometimes he even helps Wonder Woman's Super Hero team, the Justice League!

Etta Candy

Steve introduced Diana to many people in America, including military officer Etta Candy. Diana was impressed by Etta's humour and bravery, and soon the two women were best friends.

Sometimes, Etta joins Wonder Woman on her adventures. Etta doesn't have superpowers, but she does know how to fight, think fast and act courageously. She and Wonder Woman make a great team.

Wonder Woman still misses her friends from Themyscira and always enjoys a chance to visit home. However, she's so happy to have Etta, who will always be there for her with great advice and terrible jokes.

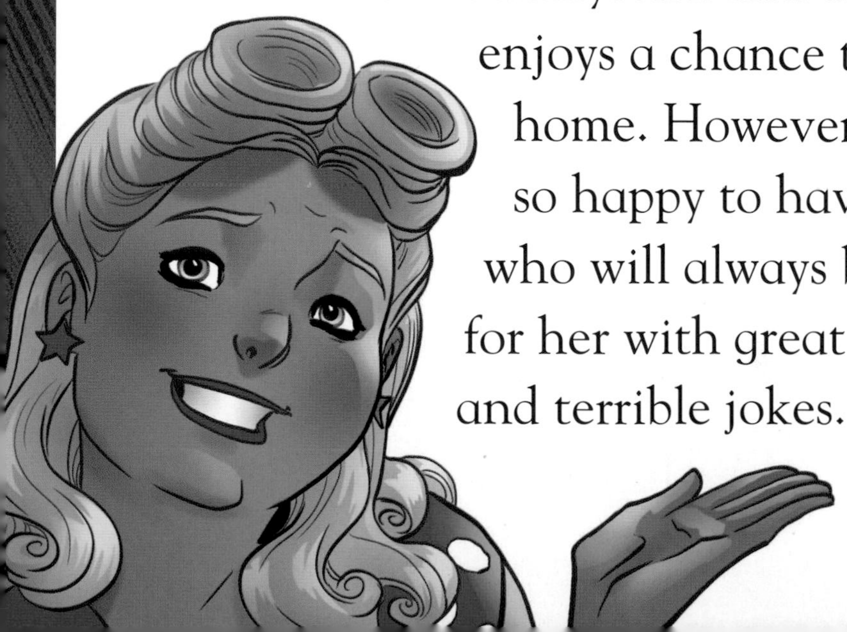

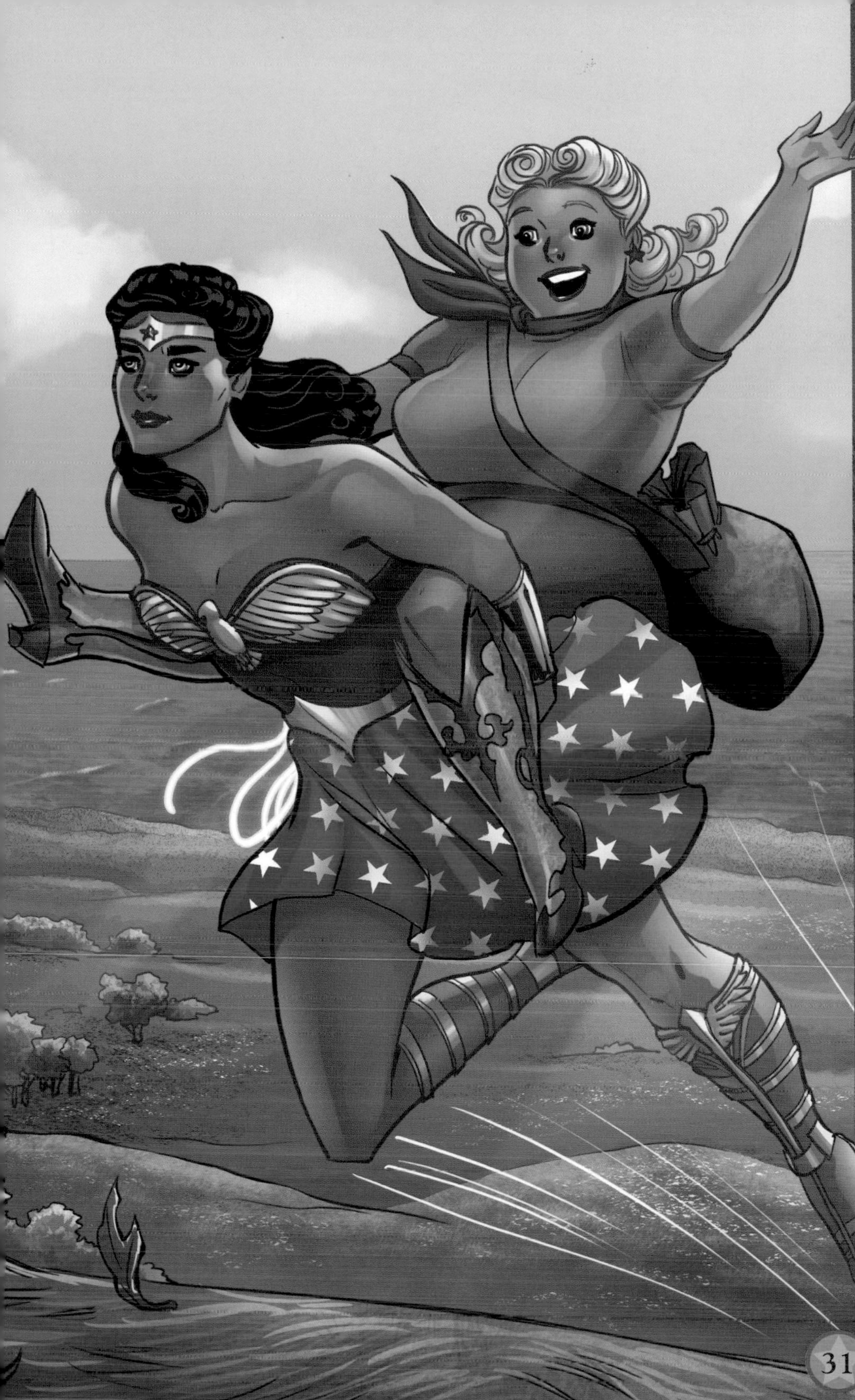

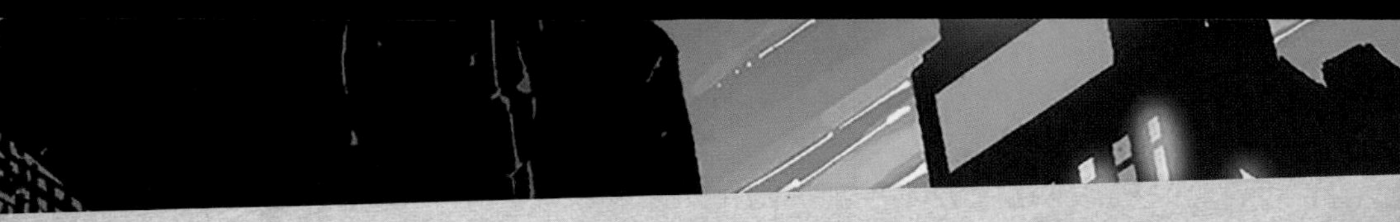

DAILY PLANET

SPECIAL EDITION

AMAZON PRINCESS ARRIVES IN AMERICA

People all over the globe were shocked to learn that a previously unknown island in the middle of the ocean is home to a tribe of immortal women. And they were thrilled to hear that one of those women has decided to live among them... as a Super Hero!

Wonder Woman, princess of the island known as Themyscira, comes from a land that humankind and modern technology have never touched. Her people, the Amazons, have only ever known peace. Clearly, they could teach us a thing or two.

But Diana hasn't just come to teach; she has also come to learn. "So many things here

VOWS TO HELP HUMANITY!

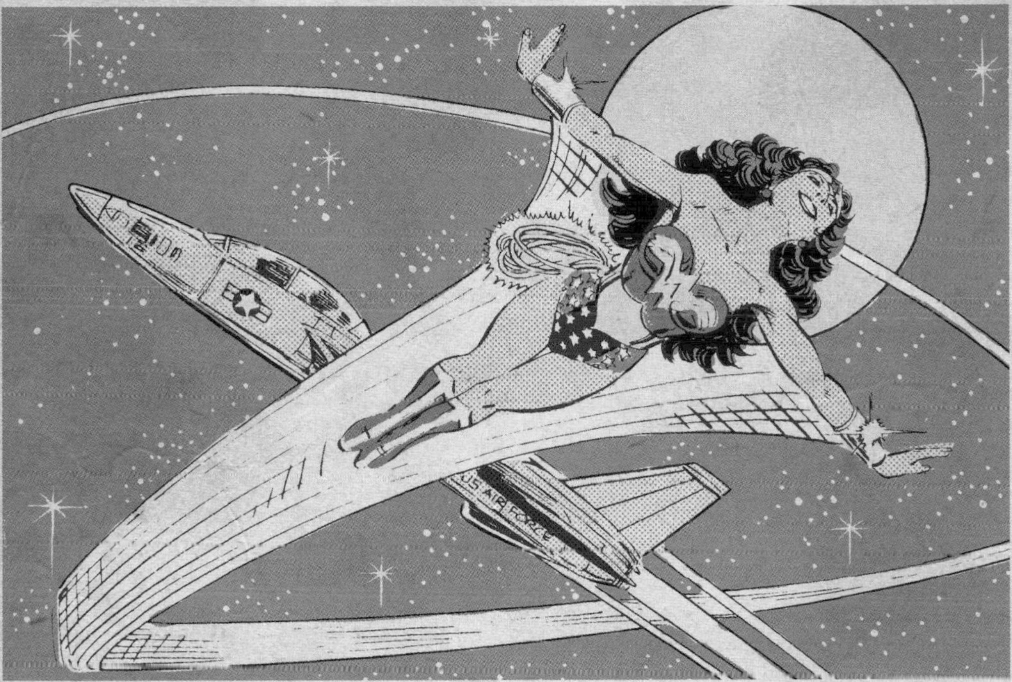
US AIR FORCE

are unfamiliar", she says of our world, "and so many of them are beautiful".

The greatest surprise of all, of course, is that Diana is not just a princess, and not just an ambassador: she also has a huge range of superpowers to rival any hero or villain. She can fly, lift thousands of pounds and hear a pin drop from a mile away. She speaks at least a hundred languages, and that number grows daily.

With Diana's arrival, the world became a little more wonderful this week.

Sidekicks

Donna Troy and Wonder Woman began as enemies. Donna was created by an evil sorceress as a replacement for Wonder Woman. After fighting – and losing to – Diana, Donna thought hard about her life. She decided to betray her creator, become the Super Hero Wonder Girl and fight beside the woman she was made to destroy.

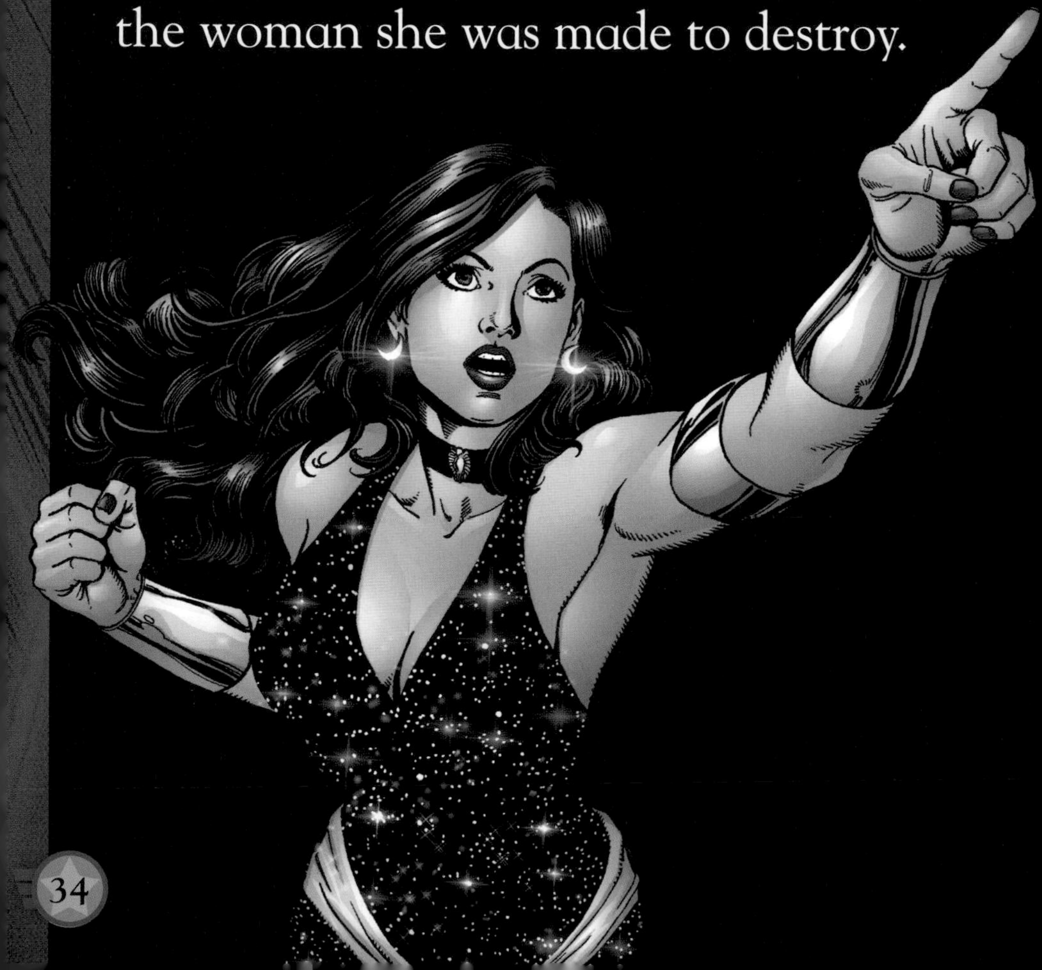

Cassie Sandsmark was a normal teenager – until she activated a magical antique. In the adventures that followed, she met Wonder Woman, and she was later granted superpowers by the god Zeus. Now she is a member of the Super Hero group Teen Titans, and fights crime as the second Wonder Girl!

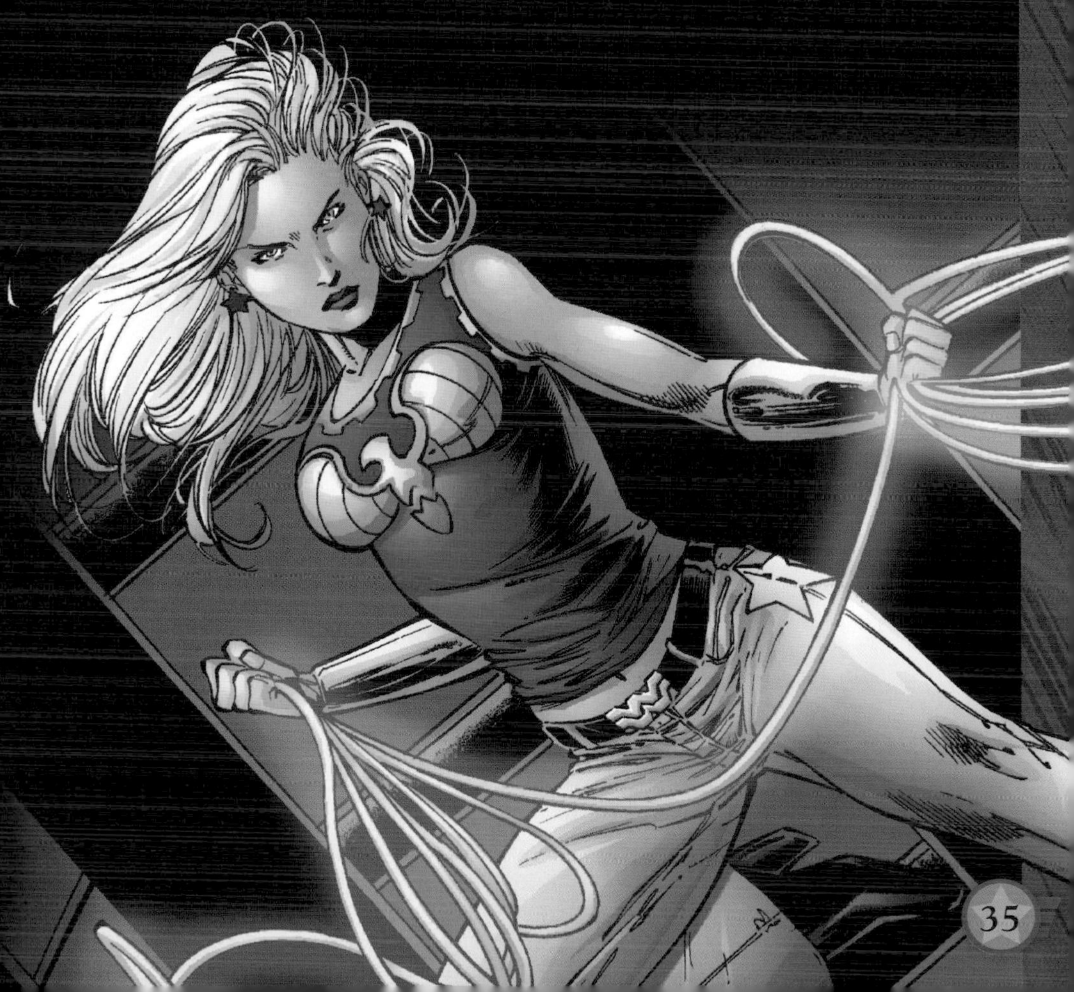

Cheetah

Barbara Minerva was an archaeologist and an expert in old weapons. One day she cut herself on a cursed knife. The magic of the knife transformed her into a half-woman, half-cheetah and it granted her surprising speed and strength. But the evil knife also made Barbara violent and greedy. She became the super-villain Cheetah!

Cheetah remembers her fondness for old and rare weapons, and so she is obsessed with

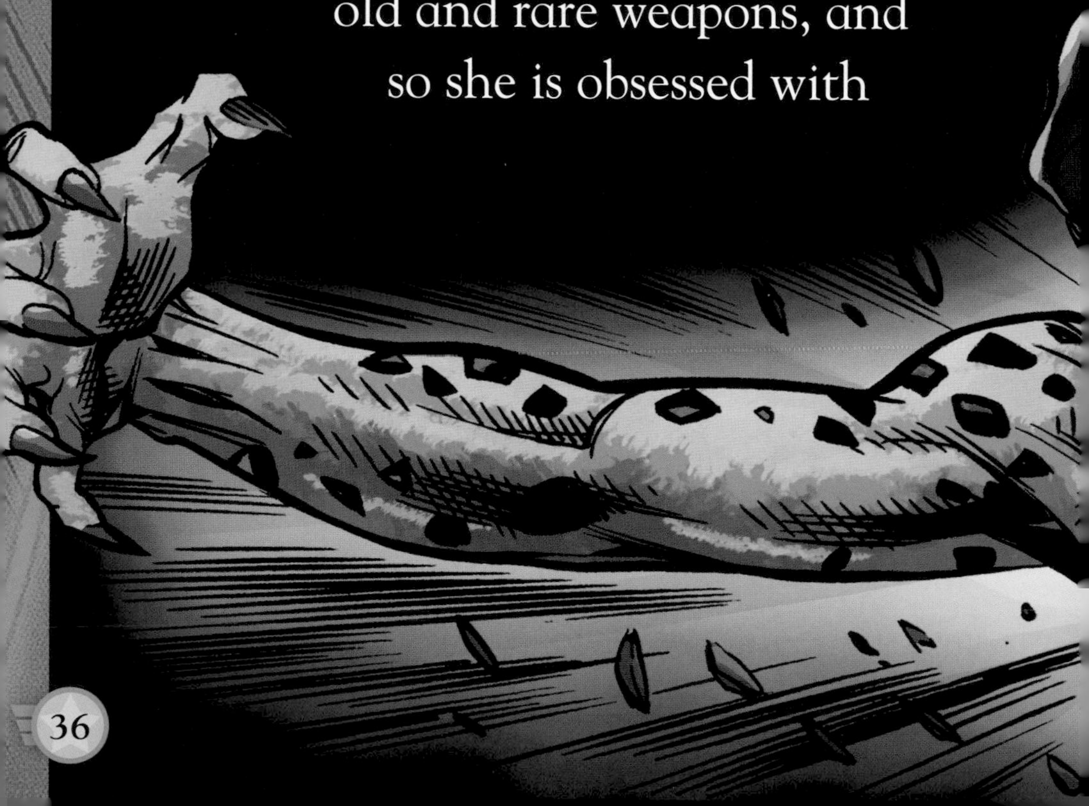

Wonder Woman's lasso. She has tried to steal the lasso countless times and considers Wonder Woman her greatest enemy.

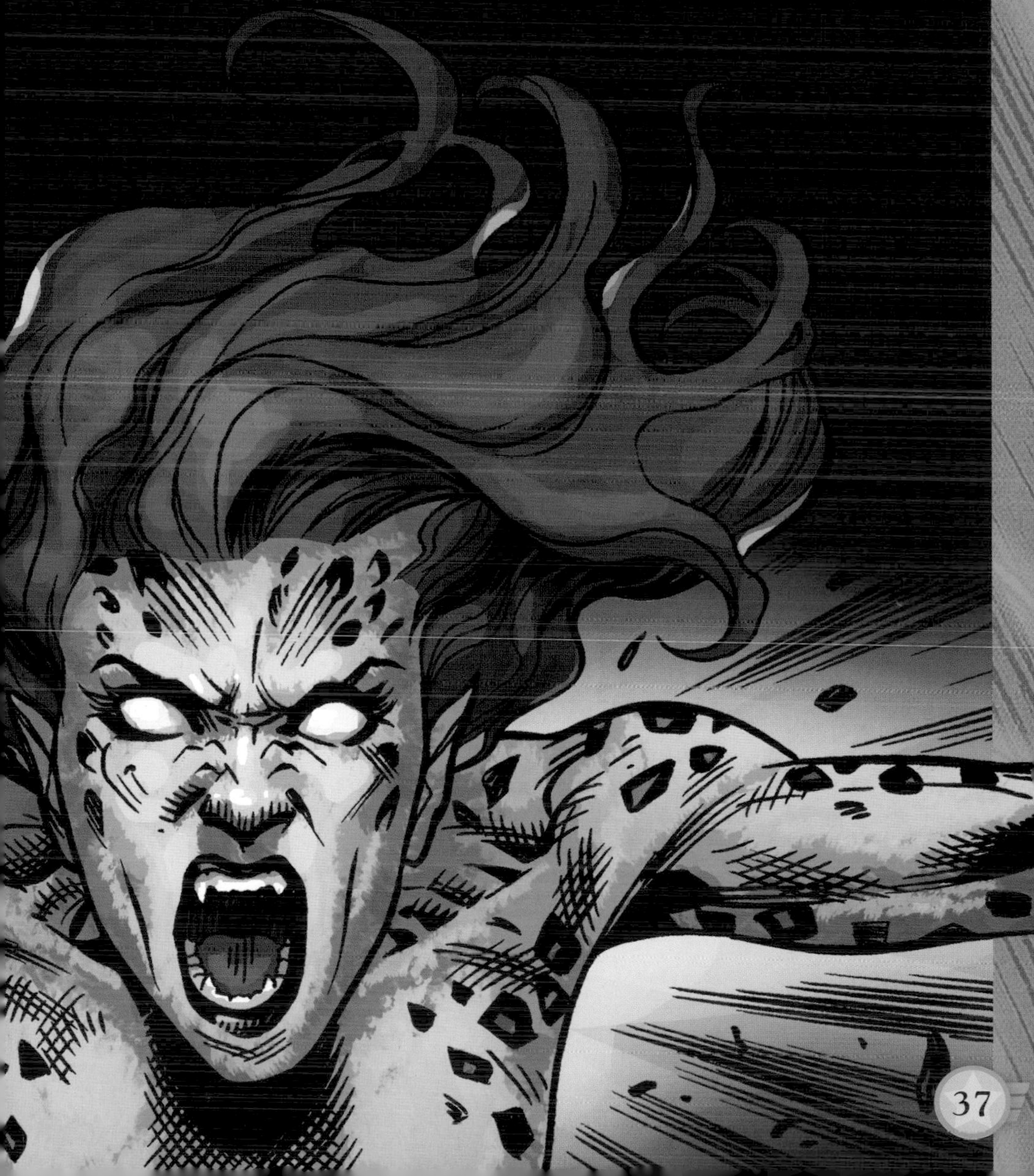

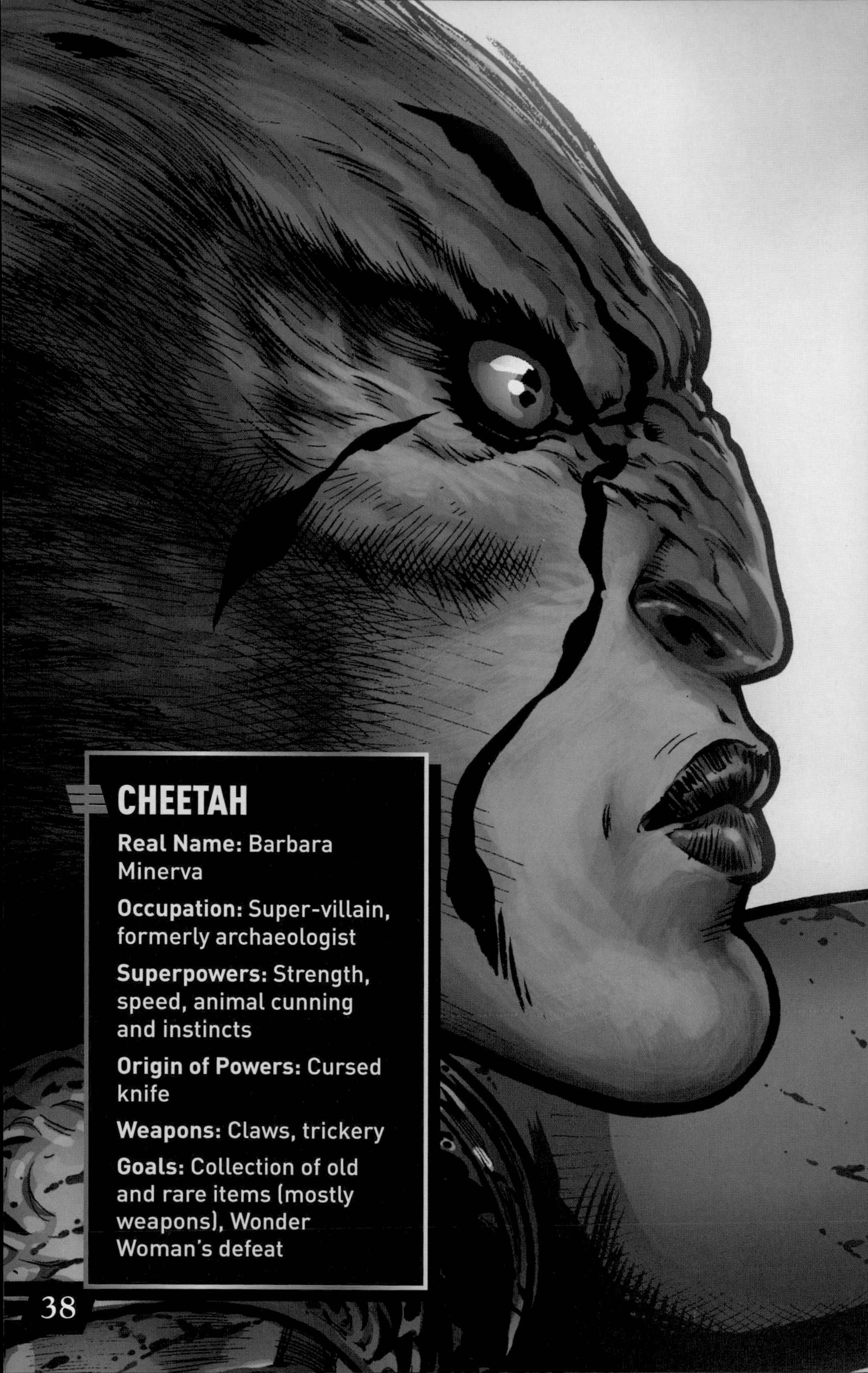

CHEETAH

Real Name: Barbara Minerva

Occupation: Super-villain, formerly archaeologist

Superpowers: Strength, speed, animal cunning and instincts

Origin of Powers: Cursed knife

Weapons: Claws, trickery

Goals: Collection of old and rare items (mostly weapons), Wonder Woman's defeat

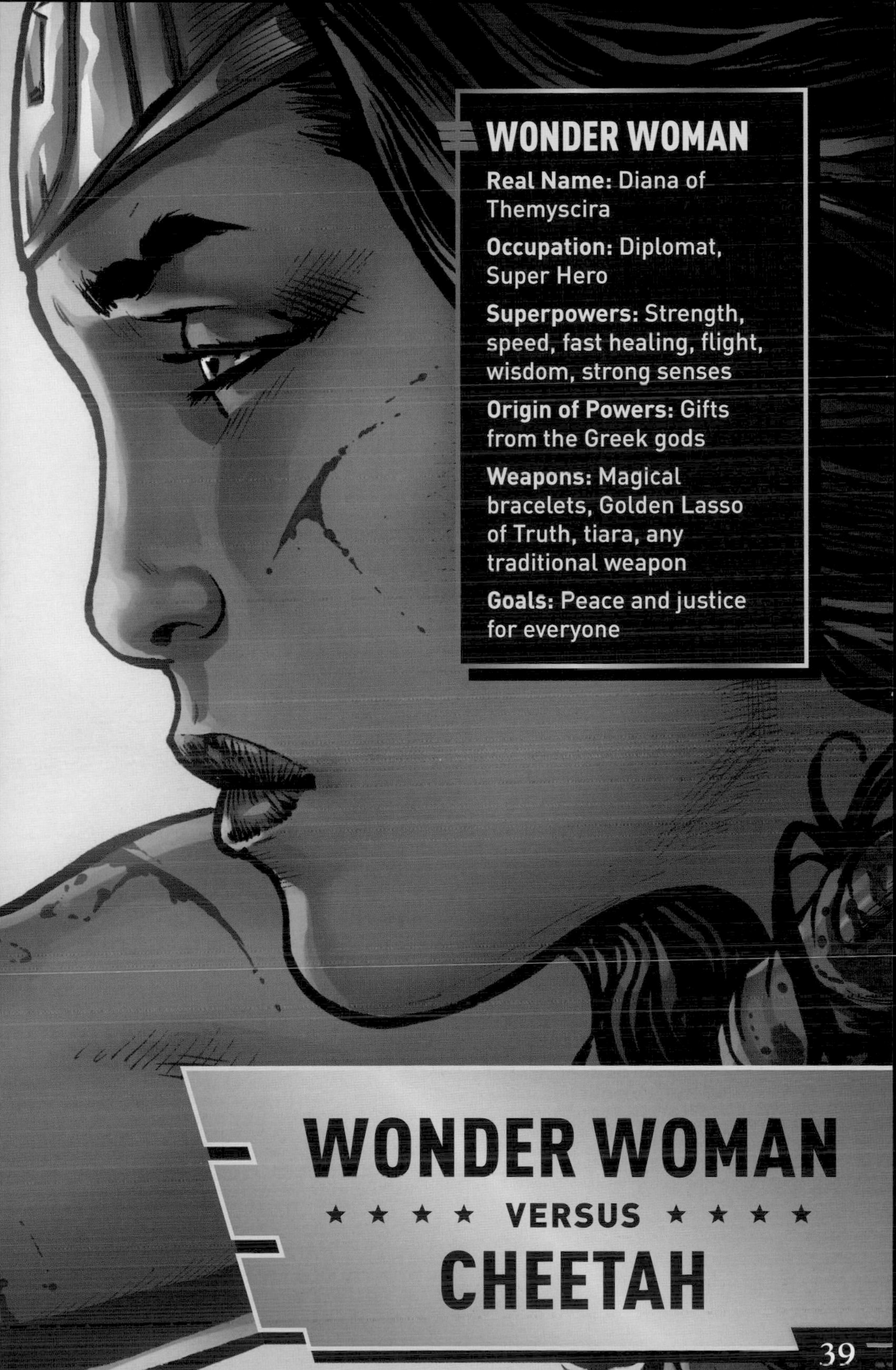

WONDER WOMAN

Real Name: Diana of Themyscira

Occupation: Diplomat, Super Hero

Superpowers: Strength, speed, fast healing, flight, wisdom, strong senses

Origin of Powers: Gifts from the Greek gods

Weapons: Magical bracelets, Golden Lasso of Truth, tiara, any traditional weapon

Goals: Peace and justice for everyone

WONDER WOMAN

★ ★ ★ ★ VERSUS ★ ★ ★ ★

CHEETAH

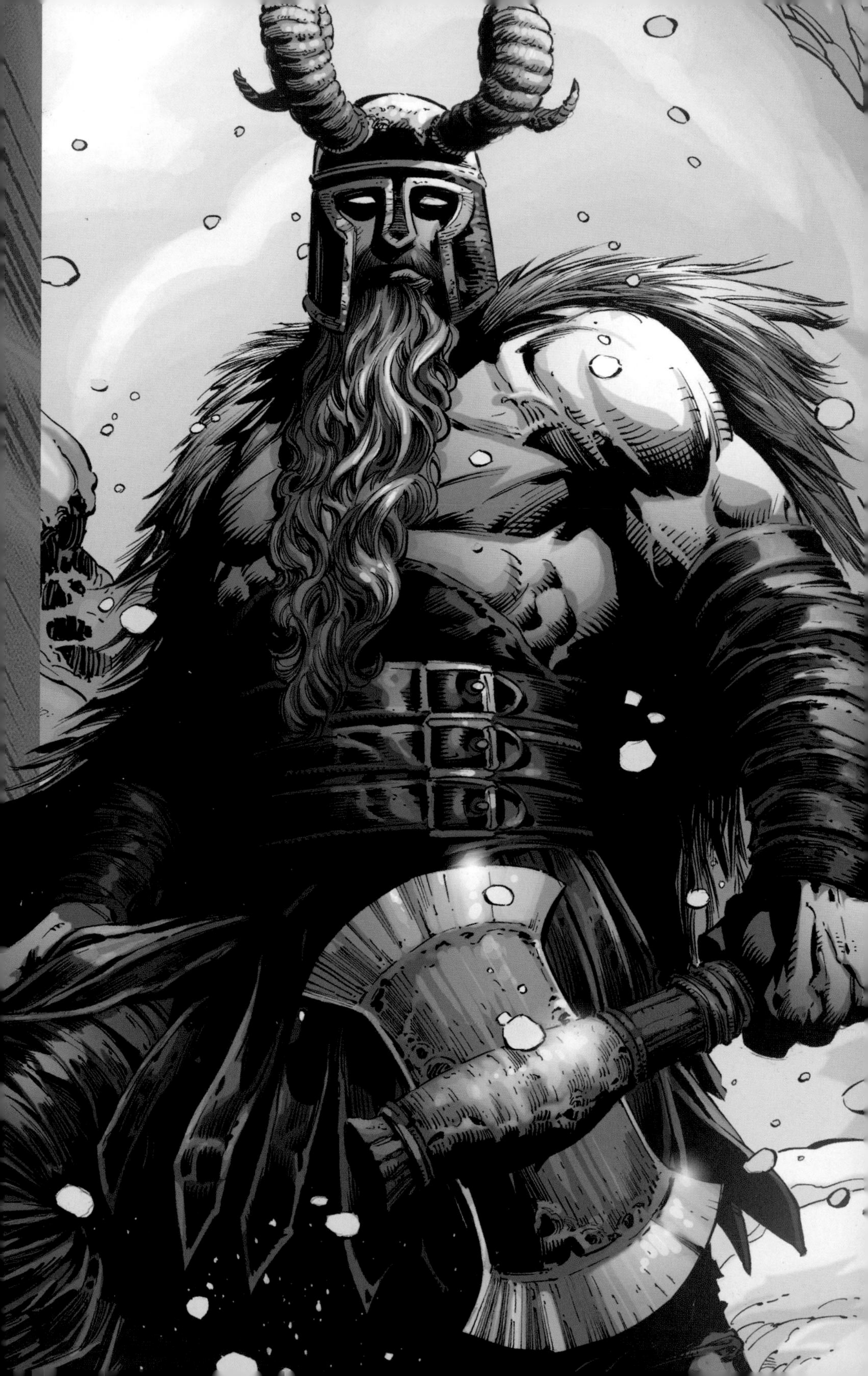

The God of War

Not all the Greek gods agreed to create peace-loving Paradise Island. Ares (Air-eez), the Greek god of war, hates what the Amazons stand for. He hates Wonder Woman even more, since she has left the island and is spreading her peaceful message to the world.

As a god, Ares is a frightening enemy to have. He is just as strong and fast as Wonder Woman. He is a master of strategy, so his plans to

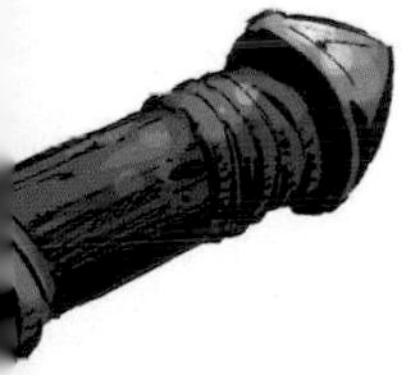

beat Wonder Woman are crafty and complicated. Because he is the god of war, any anger or violence around him makes him stronger.

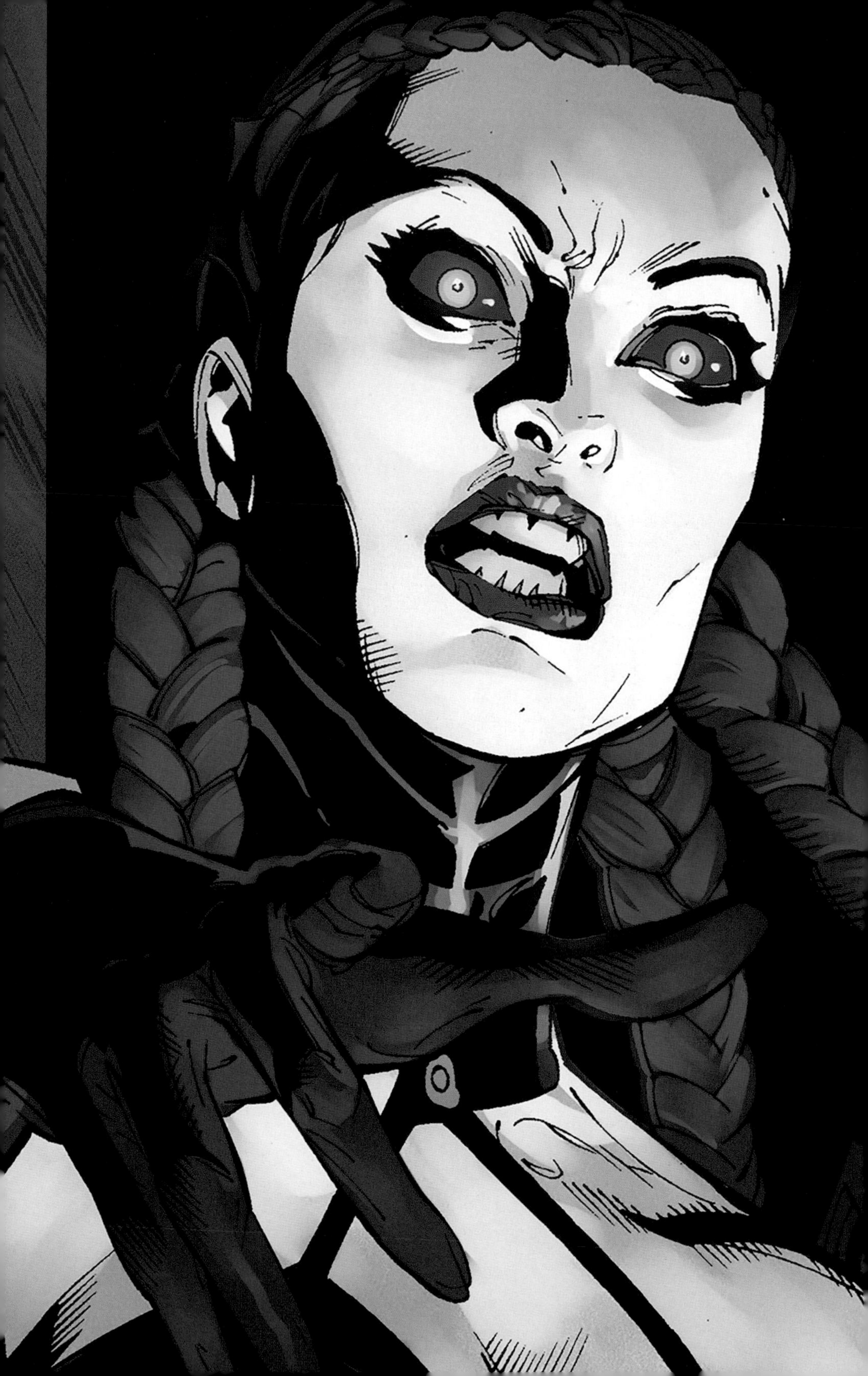

Circe

Circe (Sur-see) is a very evil and very powerful sorceress. Her magic is strong because she is related to the Greek gods. With her powers, she can do nearly anything she can imagine. And since Circe loves to embarrass and upset people, Wonder Woman always tries to stop her.

Circe can stay alive forever and give herself superpowers to match Wonder Woman's. She can change any object into another object: land into water, air into stone, people into animals. She can even change people's memories! It takes everything Wonder Woman has to keep this terrible villain under control.

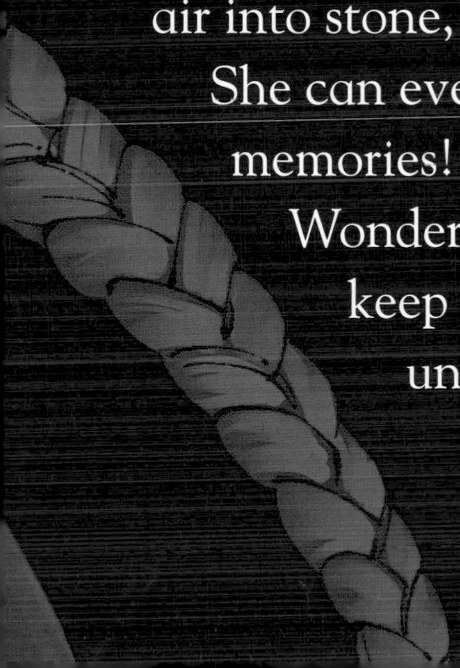

Giganta

Doctor Doris Zuel was a brilliant scientist who wanted to perform dangerous experiments. She captured Wonder Woman and tried to put her own mind into Wonder Woman's body. When that failed, Dr Zuel continued doing crazy experiments on herself until she gained the ability to grow hundreds of feet tall.

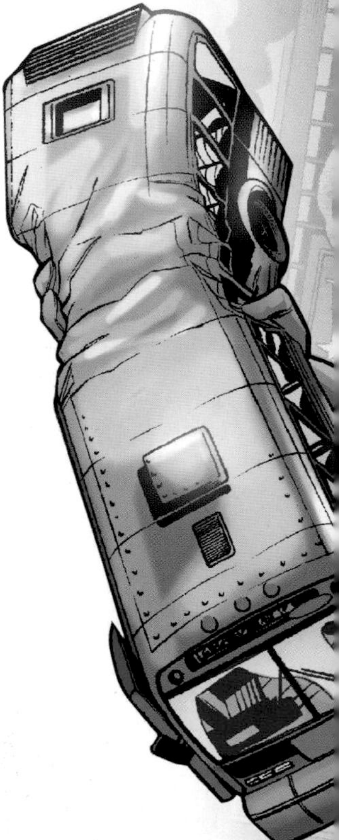

As the villain Giganta, Dr Zuel can change her size whenever she wants. This evil genius has designed a special bulletproof suit that grows and shrinks with her. When she is huge, she is also extremely strong. This super-villain is a gigantic challenge for Wonder Woman!

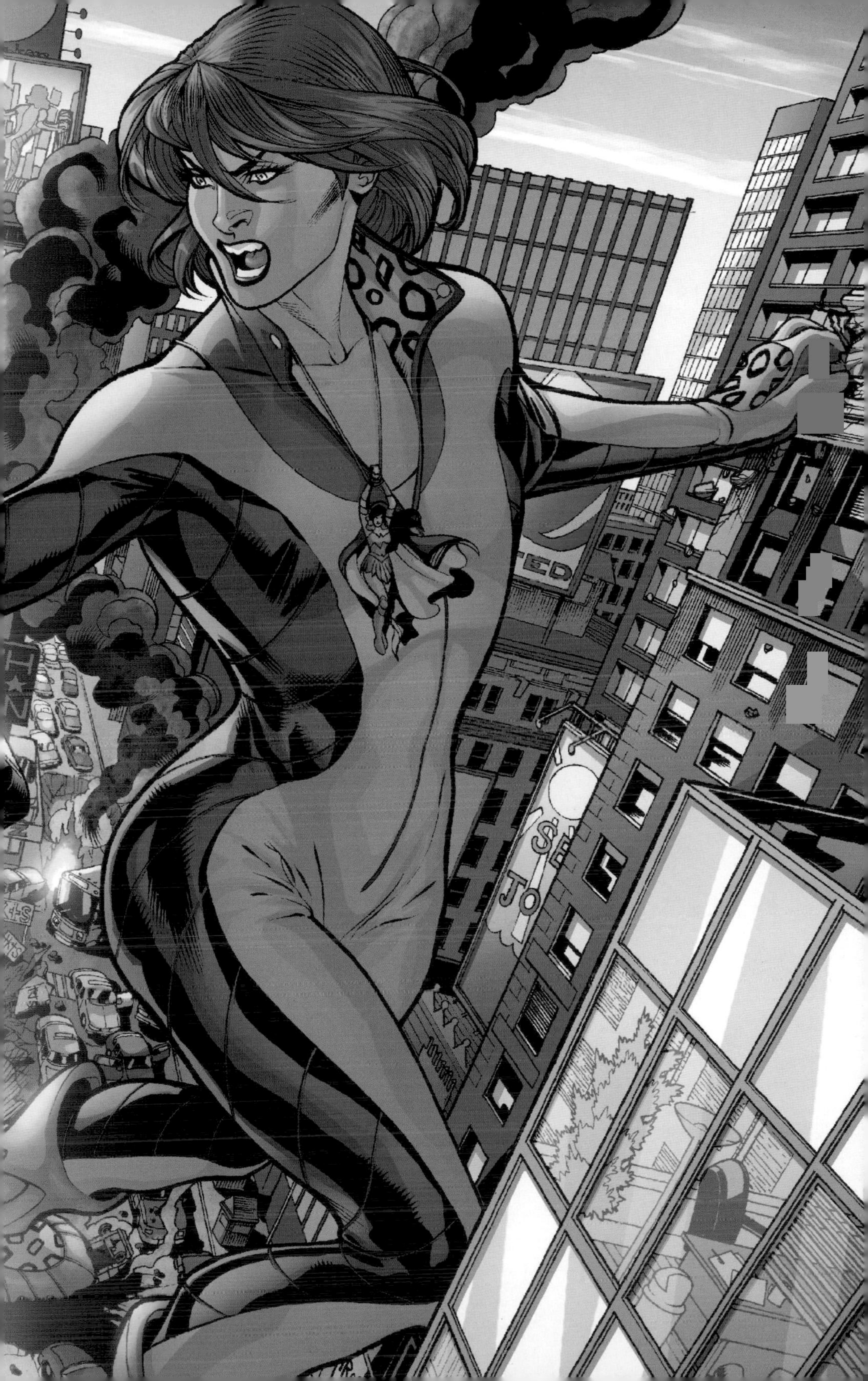

The Man of Steel

There are times when Wonder Woman works with other Super Heroes. She often fights side by side with an alien named Superman. Born on a planet called Krypton, he was raised on Earth after his planet exploded. He looks just like a human, but he has many amazing abilities. He uses his powers to keep people safe, especially the people of his home city, Metropolis.

Superman and Wonder Woman have

a lot in common. They both fight for justice and peace. They both come from places that most people had never heard of before. They even have some of the same superpowers!

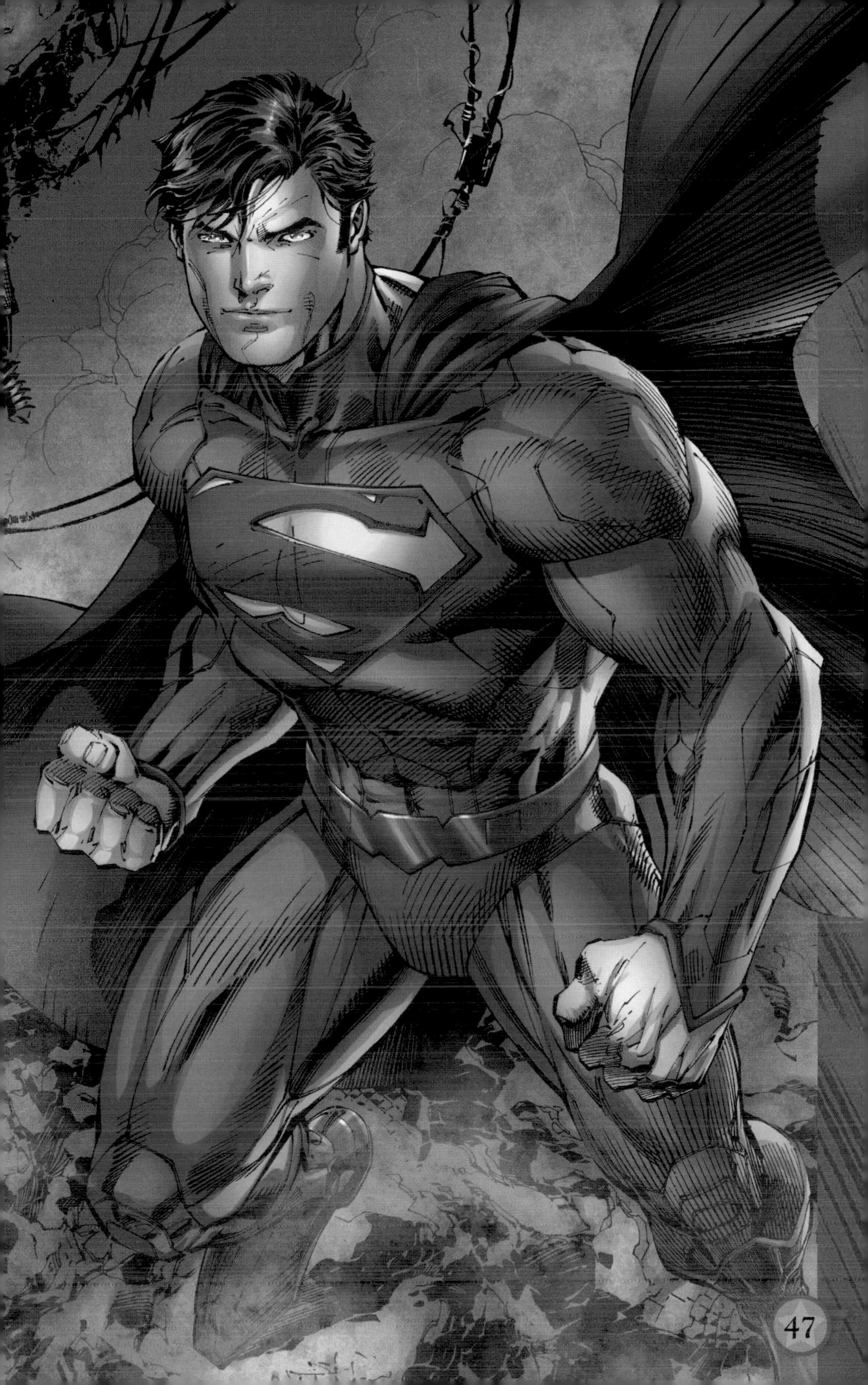

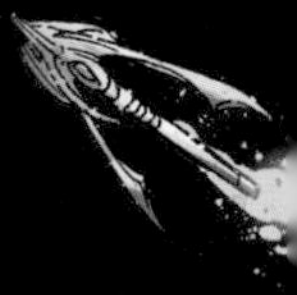

The Dark Knight

Wonder Woman does not have much in common with another Super Hero – Batman, the protector of Gotham City. Instead of inspiring people to be better, like Wonder Woman, Batman scares them into being good. Wonder Woman doesn't mind people seeing her, but Batman prefers to travel under the cover of night. Batman has no superpowers – instead, he trains to be as strong and fast as a human can possibly be.

Batman also builds gadgets and vehicles to help him. For instance, he can't fly like Wonder Woman, but he can pilot his high-tech Batplane.

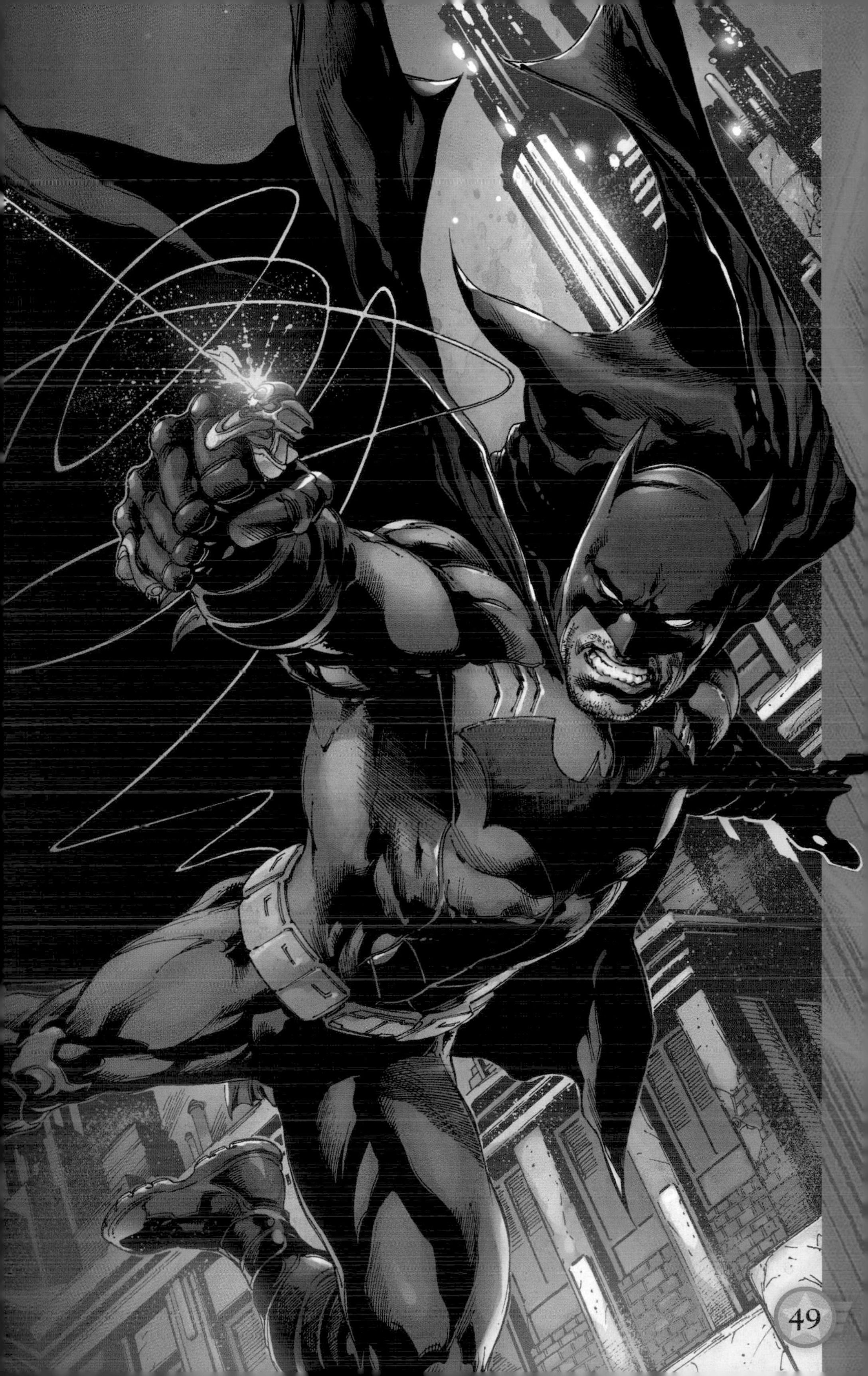

THE TRINITY
Superman, Batman and Wonder Woman

Wonder Woman, Batman and Superman are the most powerful Super Heroes on Earth! They all fight for justice, but they do it in different ways and for different reasons.

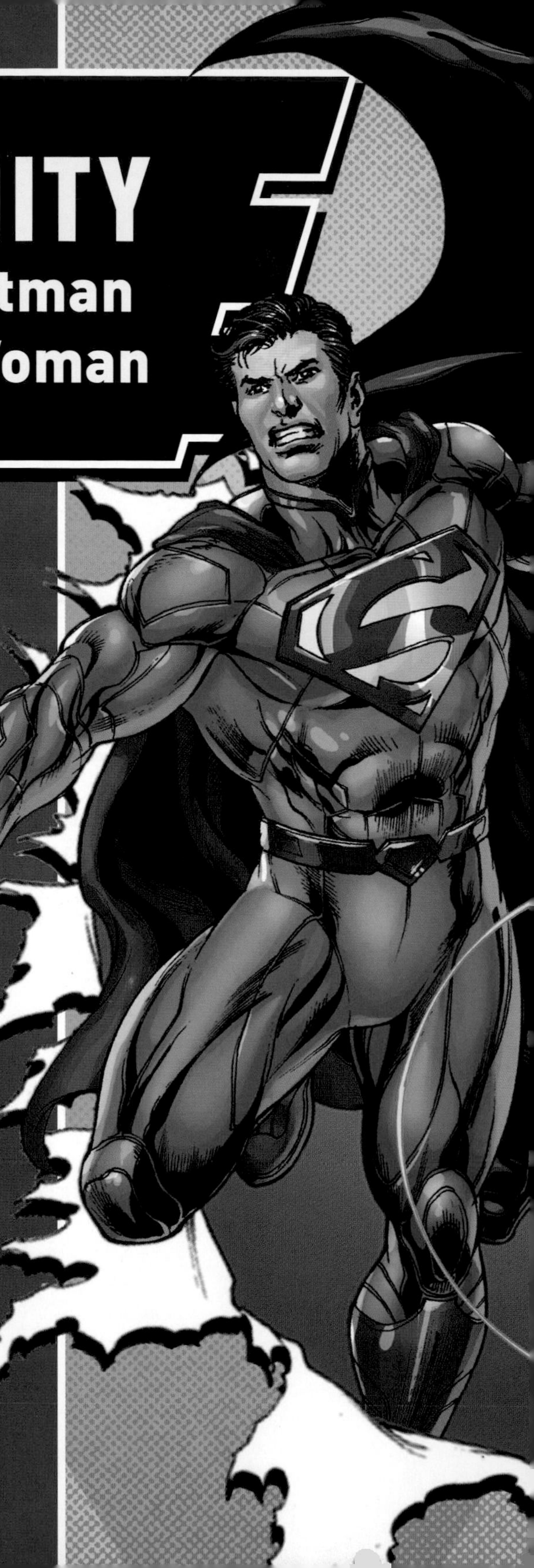

SUPERMAN

Kryptonian Name: Kal-El

Human Name: Clark Kent

Nicknames: The Man of Steel, Big Blue

Occupation: Newspaper reporter

Abilities: Strength, speed, flight, heat vision, freeze breath, super-hearing, X-ray vision

Became a Super Hero to: Use his Kryptonian powers for good

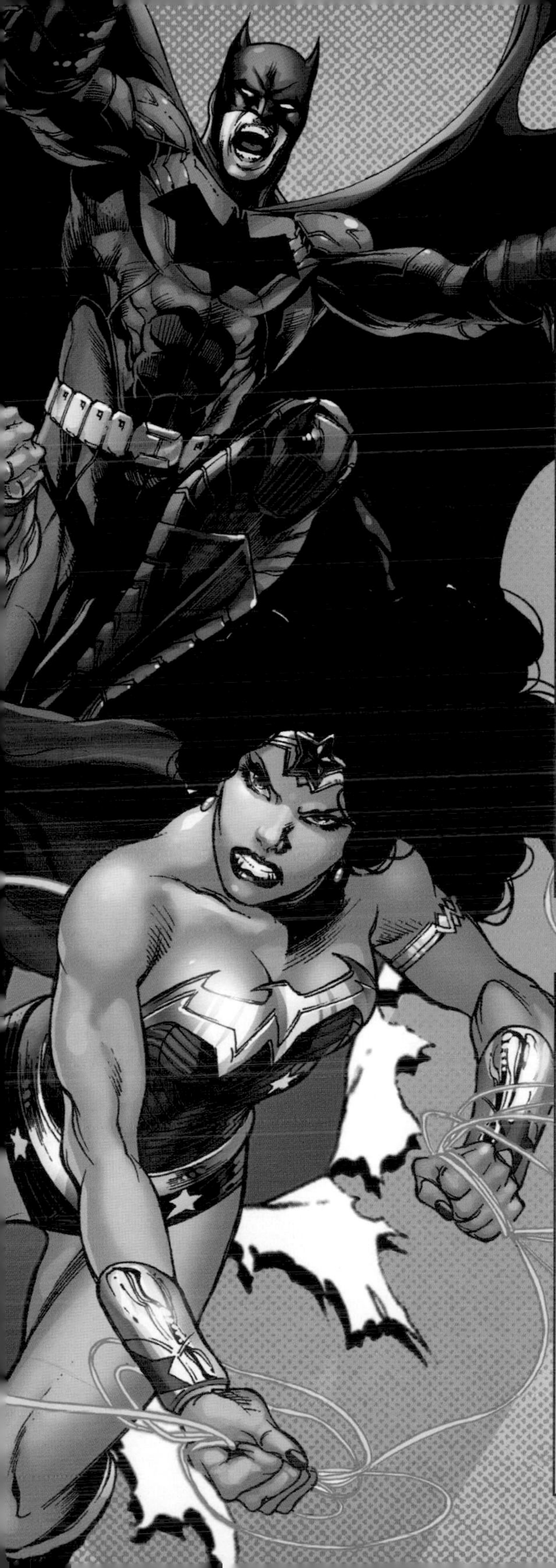

BATMAN

Real Name: Bruce Wayne

Nicknames: The Caped Crusader, the Dark Knight

Occupation: Billionaire business owner

Abilities: Genius, hand-to-hand combat and martial arts, detective skills, inventing and building many special tools, gadgets and vehicles

Became a Super Hero to: Protect people from criminals like the ones who killed his parents

WONDER WOMAN

Real Name: Diana of Themyscira

Nicknames: The Amazing Amazon, Wondy

Occupation: Diplomat

Abilities: Strength, speed, fast healing, flight, wisdom, super senses, diplomacy, strategy

Became a Super Hero to: Teach people to be peaceful and fair

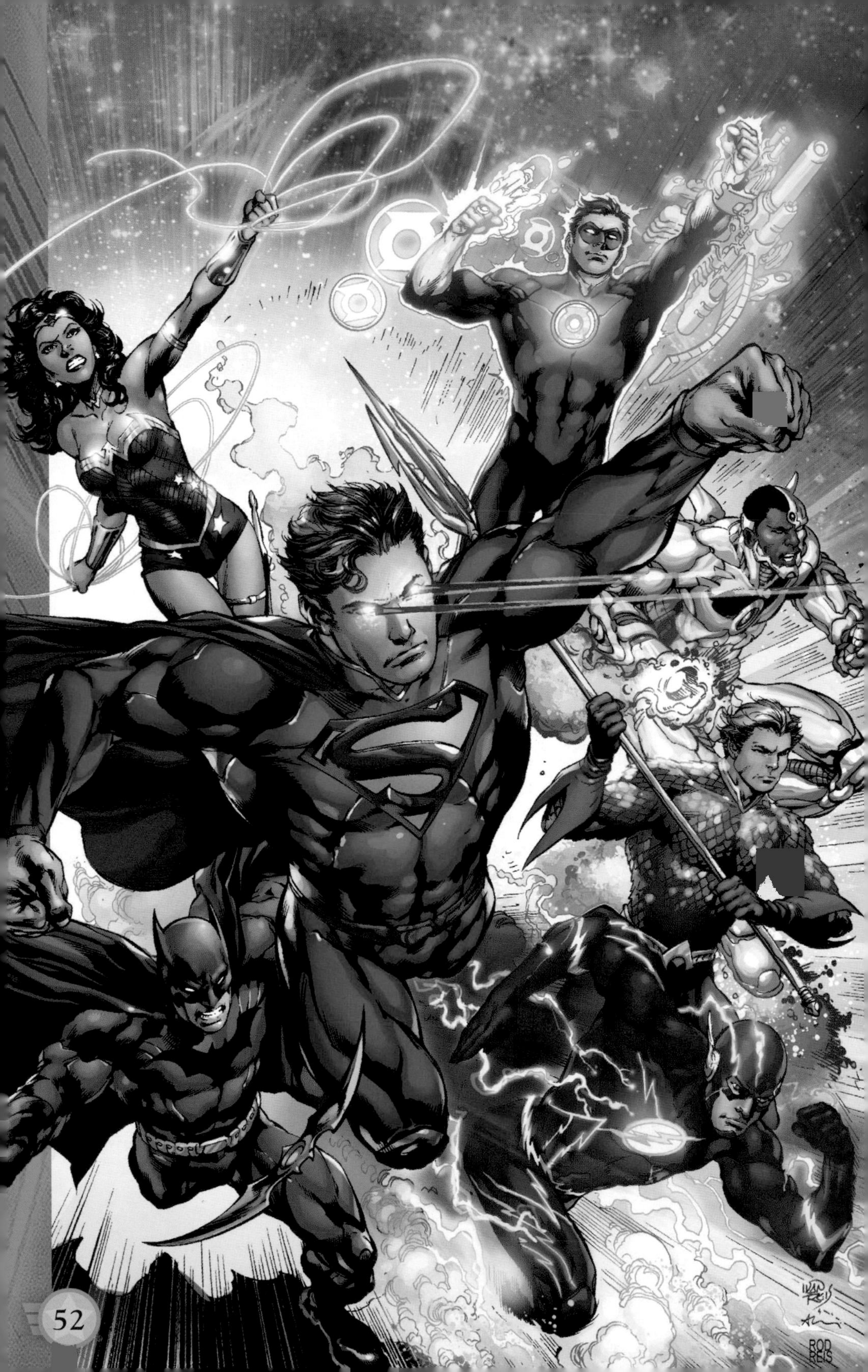
ROD REIS

The Justice League

Superman, Batman and Wonder Woman are all very strong Super Heroes. On their own, they can easily handle most criminals. However, sometimes a villain appears who is so dangerous, no Super Hero can stop them alone.

That's when it's time to team up! Earth's mightiest Super Heroes have joined together to form one incredible super group. Separately, they are Superman, Batman, Wonder Woman, Aquaman, Green Lantern, the Flash and Cyborg. Together, they are the Justice League! This amazing team has saved the planet many times. They can take down any enemy, or even a whole team of villains!

THE FLASH

Real Name: Barry Allen

Occupation: Scientist

After being struck by lightning while handling dangerous chemicals, Barry Allen became the Fastest Man Alive. The Flash can move faster than the speed of light, which also allows him to learn and heal very quickly.

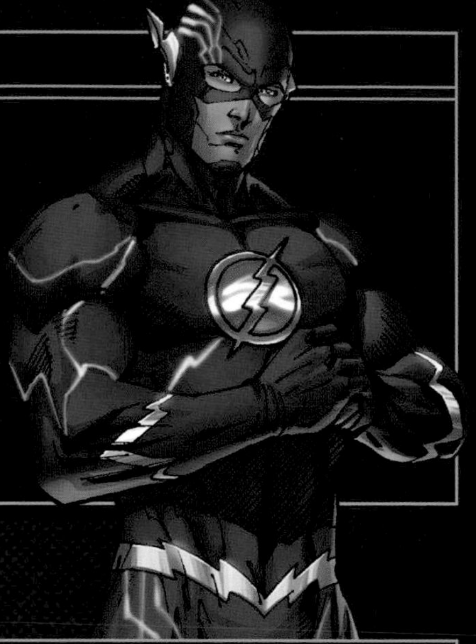

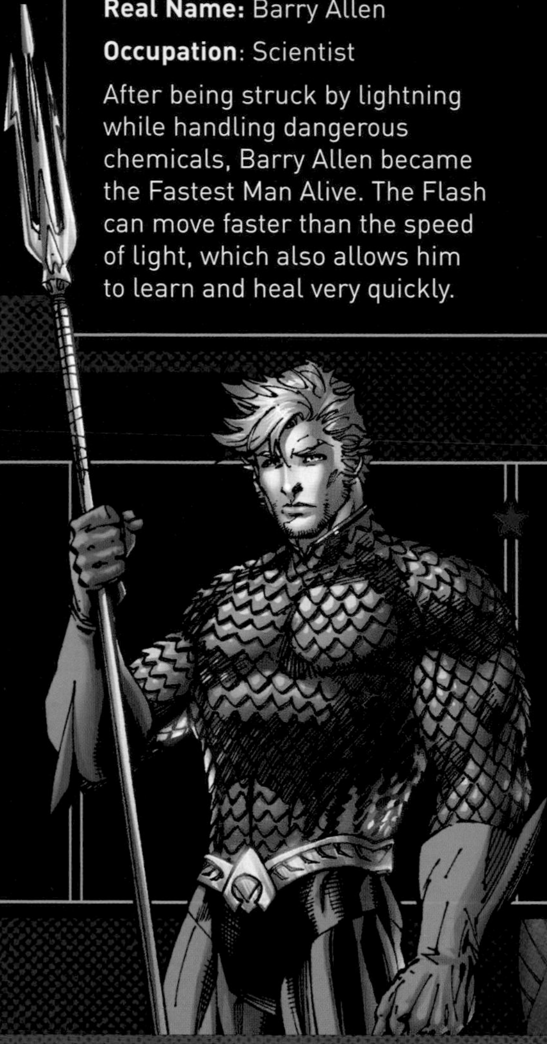

AQUAMAN

Real Name: Arthur Curry

Occupation: King of Atlantis

Aquaman is the son of a human father and a mother from the underwater kingdom of Atlantis. He is super-strong, can live underwater and can talk with any creature that lives in the ocean.

JUSTICE LEAGUE ROLL CALL

Who's Who in the Hall of Justice

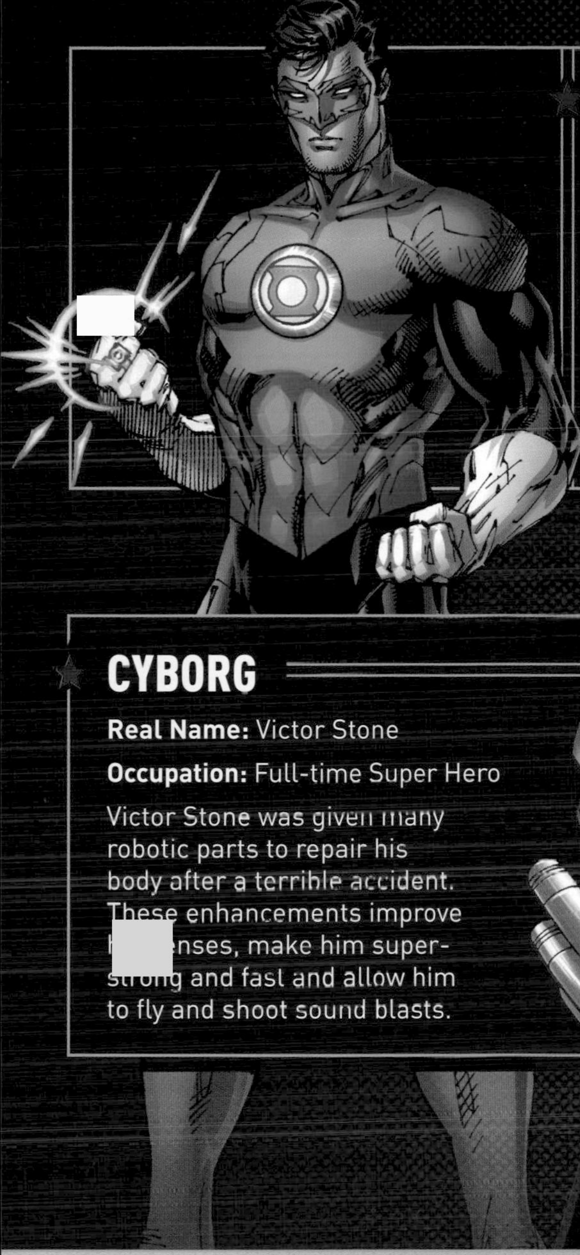

GREEN LANTERN

Real Name: Hal Jordan

Occupation: Pilot

Fearless test pilot Hal Jordan was chosen to join the Green Lantern Corps, an intergalactic police force. With his power ring, Green Lantern can fly, resist damage and make any shape he can imagine out of light.

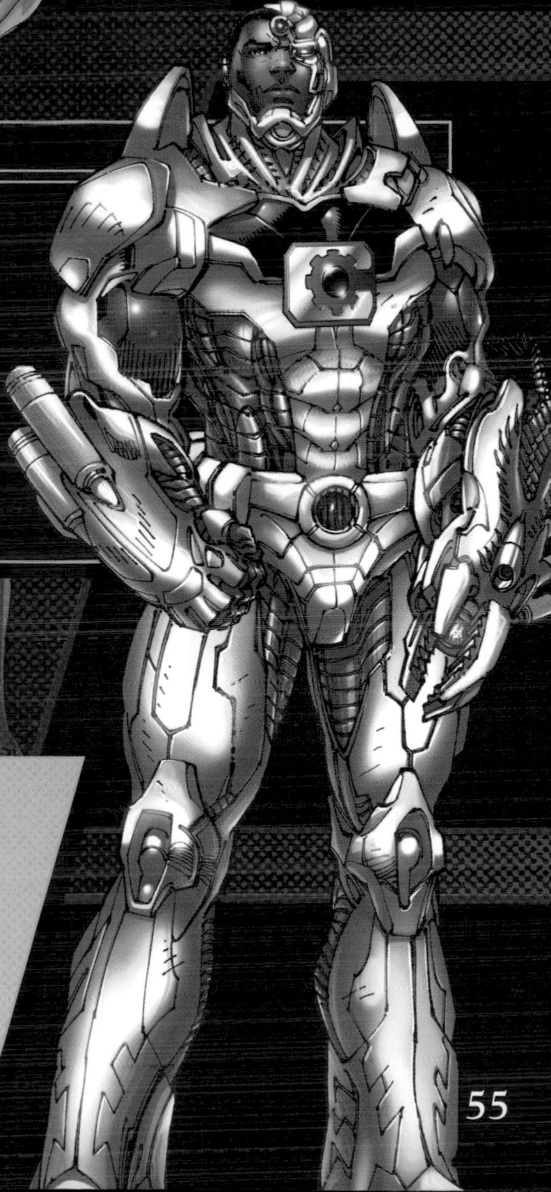

CYBORG

Real Name: Victor Stone

Occupation: Full-time Super Hero

Victor Stone was given many robotic parts to repair his body after a terrible accident. These enhancements improve h[illegible]nses, make him super-strong and fast and allow him to fly and shoot sound blasts.

Wonder Woman's role in the Justice League gives her the chance to work alongside all kinds of unusual Super Heroes!

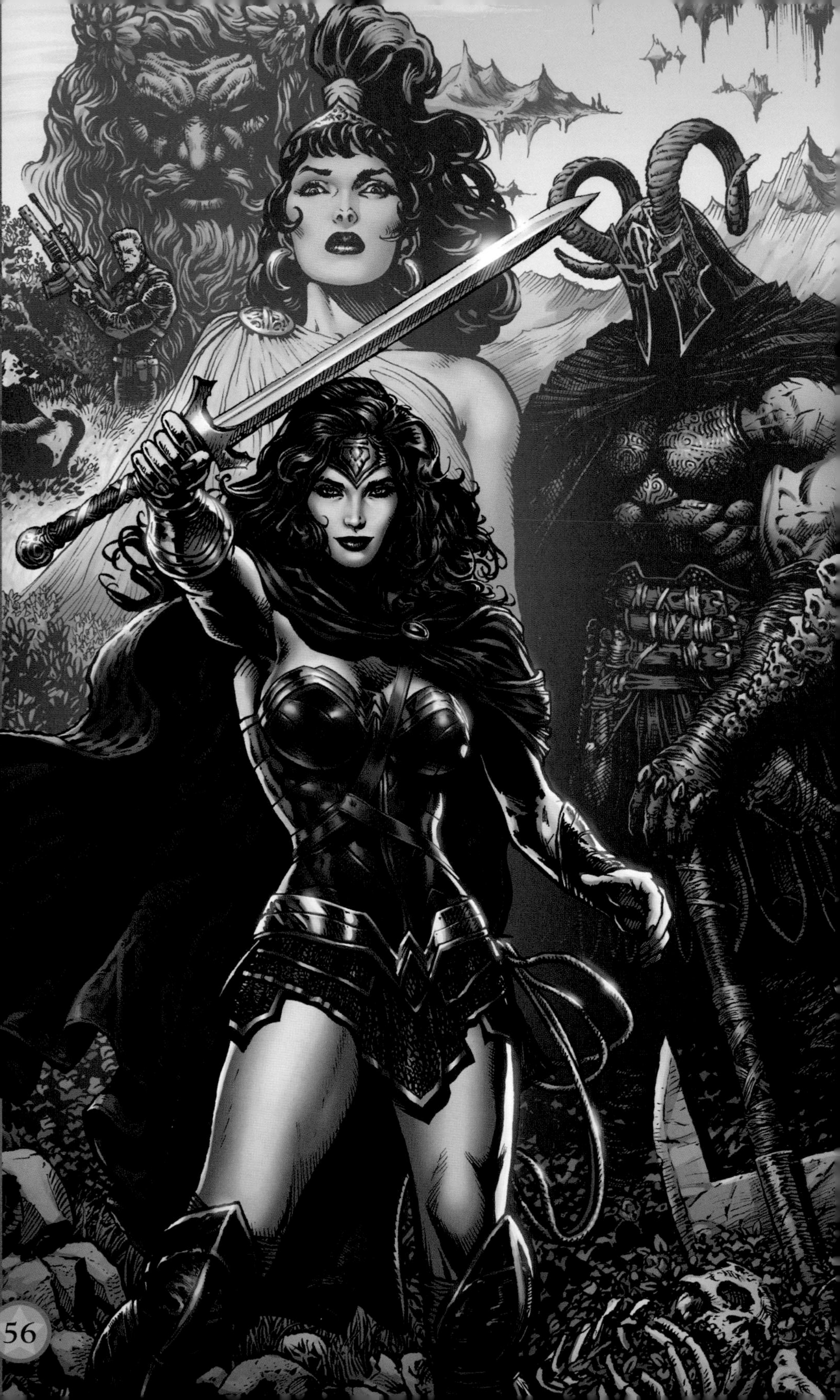

A Hero for Us All

The Amazons taught her to be fair-minded, peaceful and strong. The gods gave her superpowers, and her mother gave her a mission. Princess Diana of Themyscira went out into the world, with no idea of what she would find there.

She found lifelong friends. She found powerful enemies. She found people who needed her and other Super Heroes who would fight alongside her. Whether she's working alone, with her friends, or with her superpowered teammates, Wonder Woman is always ready to help anyone who needs it.

If you're in trouble, Wonder Woman is on your side!

Quiz

1. What is Themyscira also called?

2. What did Hippolyta ask the gods for?

3. What is Athena the goddess of?

4. What did Hephaestus make for Wonder Woman?

5. Who gave Wonder Woman the ability to fly?

6. Who is Wonder Woman's best friend?

7. What is Cassie Sandsmark's Super Hero name?

8. What is Cheetah's favourite thing to collect?

9. Which Super Hero does Wonder Woman have a lot in common with?

10. What is one of Wonder Woman's nicknames?

Answers on page 64

Glossary

Ambassador
Someone chosen to speak for a country.

Archaeologist
Someone who learns about ancient people by the things they left behind.

Blacksmith
A person who makes things with iron.

Cunning
Able to get what one wants by using tricks.

Deflect
To make something change direction.

Diplomacy
Dealing with people by understanding and respecting their feelings and needs.

Enhanced
Increased or improved.

Imaginative
Having a good imagination.

Instinct
A natural, unthinking reaction.

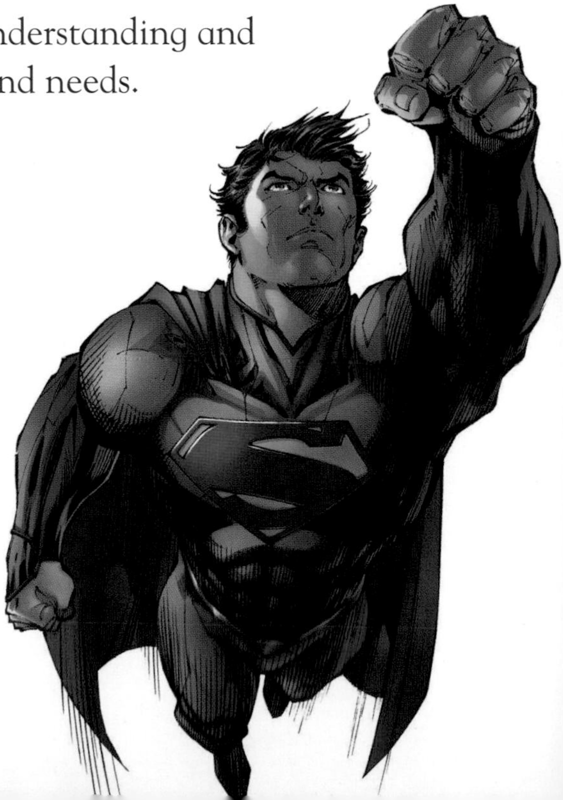

Harvest
Gathering plants that
are grown as food.

Paradise
A place where everything is perfect.

Satellite
A machine that flies around the Earth
collecting information.

Strategy
A plan for winning a fight.

Tiara
A crown.

Tournament
A series of contests where people
compete to win a prize.

Traditional
Something that has been done for
a long time.

Vibration
Small movements back and forth.

Violence
The use of physical force to hurt someone.

Guide for Parents

This book is part of an exciting four-level reading series for children, developing the habit of reading widely for both pleasure and information. These chapter books have a compelling main narrative to suit your child's reading ability. Each book is designed to develop your child's reading skills, fluency, grammar awareness and comprehension in order to build confidence and engagement when reading.

Ready for a *Level 3* book

YOUR CHILD SHOULD

- be able to read many words without needing to stop and break them down into sound parts.
- read smoothly, in phrases and with expression. By this level, your child will be beginning to read silently.
- self-correct when a word or sentence doesn't sound right.

A VALUABLE AND SHARED READING EXPERIENCE

For some children, text reading, particularly nonfiction, requires much effort, but adult participation can make this both fun and easier. So here are a few tips on how to use this book with your child.

TIP 1 Check out the contents together before your child begins:

- invite your child to check the back cover text, contents page and layout of the book and comment on it.
- ask your child to make predictions about the story.
- talk about the information your child might want to find out.

TIP 2 Encourage fluent and flexible reading:

- support your child to read in fluent, expressive phrases, making full use of punctuation and thinking about the meaning.

- help your child learn to read with expression by choosing a sentence to read aloud and demonstrating how to do this.

TIP 3 Indicators that your child is reading for meaning:

- your child will be responding to the text if he/she is self-correcting and varying his/her voice.

- your child will want to talk about what he/she is reading or is eager to turn the page to find out what will happen next.

TIP 4 Chat at the end of each chapter:

- encourage your child to recall specific details after each chapter.

- let your child pick out interesting words and discuss what they mean.

- talk about what each of you found most interesting or most important.

- ask questions about the text. These help to develop comprehension skills and awareness of the language used.

A FEW ADDITIONAL TIPS

- Read to your child regularly to demonstrate fluency, phrasing and expression; to find out or check information; and for sharing enjoyment.

- Encourage your child to reread favourite texts to increase reading confidence and fluency.

- Check that your child is reading a range of different types of material, such as poems, jokes and following instructions.

Index

Answers to the quiz on pages 58 and 59:
1. Paradise Island 2. A child 3. Wisdom 4. Her Lasso
5. Hermes 6. Etta Candy 7. Wonder Girl 8. Old weapons
9. Superman 10. The Amazing Amazon or Wondy

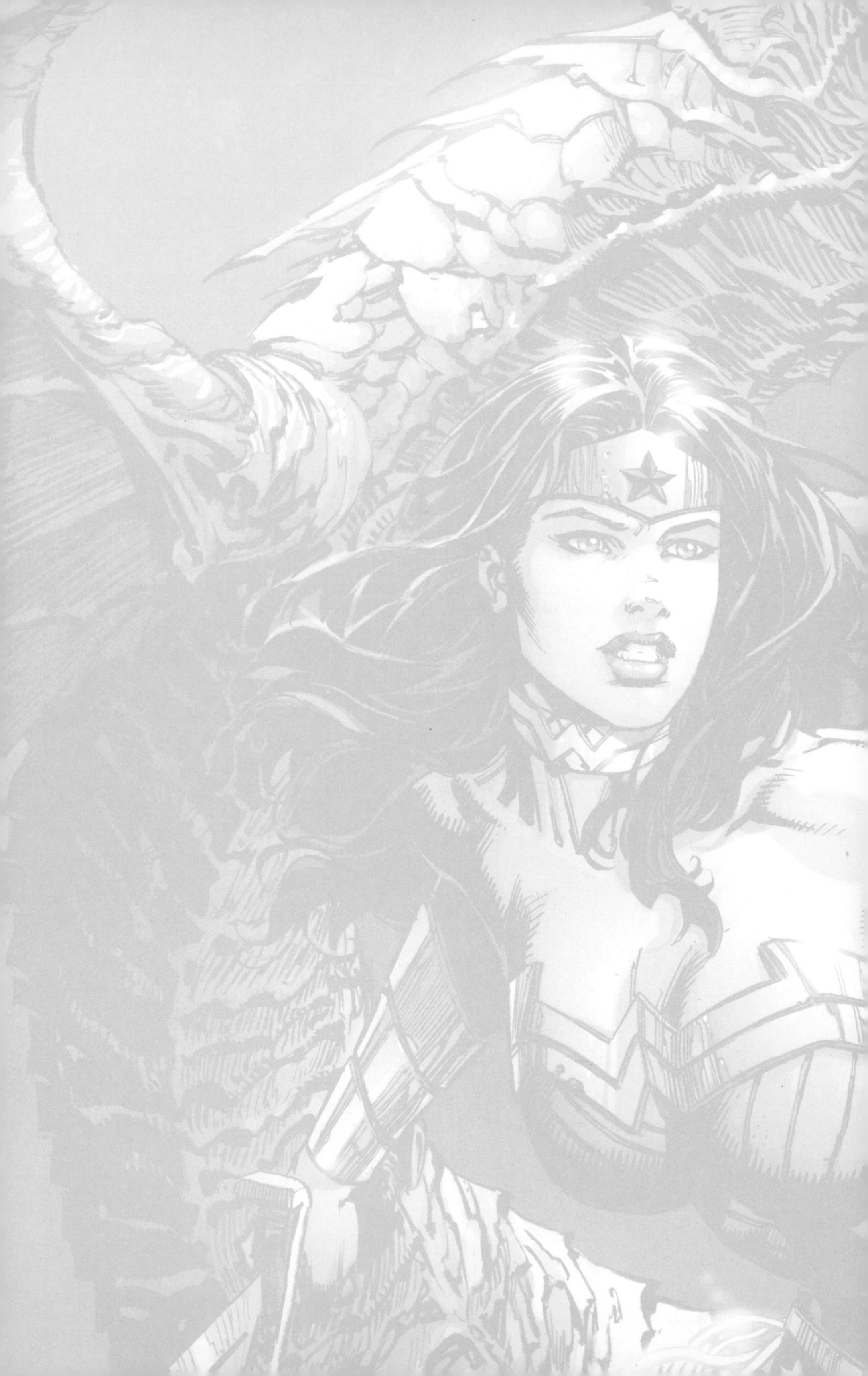